GW00993484

Choice and Change

How to Have a
Healthy Relationship with
Ourself and Others

Ches Moulton

Love & Light

Ches!

First published in 2014 by Ches Moulton

Design, typesetting and printing by:
Catalyst Image Solutions: Tel: 01992 719924

Printed on acid-free paper from managed forests. This book is printed on demand, so no copies will be remaindered or pulped.

ISBN No: 978-0-9929120-0-0

Every effort has been made to give appropriate credit to copyright holders of works cited in this publication. If there are any inadvertent omissions we apologise to those concerned. The publisher apologizes for any errors or omissions in the above list and would be grateful for notification of any corrections that should be incorporated in future reprints or editions of this book. If you are the copyright holder of any uncredited work herein, please contact us at *info@chesmoulton.com*.

The purpose of this book is to educate and entertain. The author shall have neither liability nor responsibility to any person or entity with respect to any loss or damage caused, or alleged to have been caused, directly or indirectly, by the information contained in this book.

All of the case studies and examples referred to are actual occurrences and accurate. Some identifying features of people have been modified. Some samples are composites of real people and experiences.

If you do not wish to be bound by the above, you may return this book to the place where you purchased it or to the publisher for a full refund.

Testimonials

How to Have a Healthy Relationship with Ourself and Others is both a deep and dynamic treatment of the complex topic of human behaviour - how you think, feel and act. Ches Moulton carefully explains dysfunction as well as high performance with case studies and activities and deep insight. This book is for anyone who needs to understand their motivations, seeking greater meaning and purpose and looking for a refreshing take on changing for the better. I believe this book provides a very accessible gateway to improving the human experience.

Andrew Priestley,
Grad Dip Psych, BEd.

To be free and have unconditional love is unfortunately not everyone's experience in life. This is a fantastic and well written detailed book peppered with insightful nuggets of wisdom which explains the complicated issues of co-dependency in a simple, well organised and easy to understand way. Ches gives specific examples to help the reader understand the definition, symptoms and causes which helps identify or maybe recognise in oneself or loved ones how destructive this type of relationship can be.

Unfortunately there are far too many dysfunctional families with many variations of dependency from all walks of life. Ches has vast experience in this field so from his professional experience is able to give a perfect roadmap to outline the evolving process of changing, healing and recovery which results in the reader recognising that to love oneself is your greatest gift and comes from within. This book is refreshing and perfect for individuals, couples and professional practitioners.

Sheila Steptoe,
Personal Transformation Consultant
& Author of 'Master Your Own Destiny'

Having read Ches Moulton's book I can identify with the many facets of co-dependency. I considered myself a fully functioning positive and proactive member of society who is here to support others. Yet by reading this book not only can I understand others better but more importantly can understand myself better too. You will read this book and recall many memories which unknowingly have shaped your life. This insight will give you back the control you lack and the choices to make it better. By looking at the Aggressor or the Passive proves to be the beginning of truly gaining insights into another person, and more importantly myself.

Ches tells us that 'The greatest journey is that which is taken within us'. I couldn't agree more and I would like to thank you Ches for the journey I have taken simply by reading this fascinating book.

Gill Tiney,
Be Collaboration
& Author of 'Step Up'

Contents

Acknowledgements

This book is dedicated to the many people whom I have encountered, on both their journey and my own... male and female, friend and foe, accomplice and adversary. Throughout the years there have been scores of individuals who revealed their loss, allowed me to share in their victories and have unknowingly taught me many lessons about human behaviour and development. Some of those same people and countless others have witnessed my own trials and tribulations, have offered comfort and solace, and joined in the positive energy emanating from my triumphs. To all of these individuals... I am grateful!

To Kate, from whom I learned the value of that old adage... "Attraction not Promotion" and in so doing was provided with an opportunity to have a real life.

To Sayward, in whom I have a tremendous amount of pride. She came from a negative and has turned her life into a positive. She is a constant reminder of the humility I seek.

To my parents Albert and Ruth, who sought to provide me with a comfortable childhood. My mother was a source of wisdom that only resonated within me as I matured and came to realize the value of her teachings. She cared for me when I was unable to care for myself. A perfect mother to a child!

To Richard and Shirley, and Anne, three of the most decent people I have ever met and who are committed life-long friends to whom I can say anything and not be judged. The comfort derived from that knowledge is priceless.

To Celeste, an exquisite blend of traditional and contemporary values. The only person other than myself with whom I've been able to love unreservedly. She's my world! I can't imagine life without love and I can't imagine love without her!

Special thanks to Richard Costas, John Brindley, Klementyna de Sternberg Stojalowska (Klem), and Pat Fletcher for their valuable assistance in editing and remarks. You make me look good.

Additional thanks to Andrew Priestly, for his insightful comments about the material contained herein. You make me look relevant.

Gratitude is also extended to Gill Tiney for being instrumental in putting me on the right track at the beginning. You gave me momentum.

Foreword

We live in a culture that encourages us to look outside of ourself for our own happiness. We are persuaded to apply blame and give credit to others, in the belief that they are responsible for how we feel. Societal norms consider us to be selfish and conceited if we expose any attempts to love ourself beyond minimal levels of self care and attention. We are taught to put others first, and ourself last in everything we do.

Many children suffered physical, mental and emotional abuse from parents and caregivers who had experienced similar situations in their own upbringing. These adults unknowingly passed on their own dysfunction in an attempt to act out their distress and in a convoluted way, give to their children what was given to themself, in the mistaken belief that if it was good enough for them, it was good enough for their children.

The following pages attempt to address the dysfunctional habits of people who forsake any opportunity to confront their truth, while living a destructive life, without recognizing the absurdity of what they are doing.

While much of the content may seem foreign to many readers, the concepts and examples will almost at once resonate as you begin to identify people you know and hopefully yourself, and prepare to learn what is possible and any person can achieve. It will be a guide to those who desire change and a reference to those who simply want to learn more about the human condition.

You will be able to learn new skills, draw upon your inner strength, find and grow your sense of self and self-sufficiency. The processes and calls to action will embolden you to refrain from prolonging dependence on others, to connect with your self-esteem, define your wants and needs, and will give you strength to stop allowing others to determine your reality.

While the journey by its very essence must be your own, I hope this book will provide you with direction, encouragement and inspiration.

Understanding and adopting the truths contained herein will equip you with skills that will enable you to determine your own worth and endow you with the tools necessary to manage and maintain the changes required to have a healthy relationship with yourself and others.

All that is required of you after commitment has been established is honesty, open-mindedness and willingness.

H.C. Moulton DHP CH.t CSH
Brentwood
England

Preface

The first thing to do is define the concept of codependency. As the word indicates, it is a dependency between two or more people in a relationship. The relationship does not have to be a love relationship. It can be any type of relationship. For example, one between family members, friends, work mates or neighbours, to name just a few.

Of course the next question that needs to be answered is: Who is a co-dependent? The answer is contained in the description of a codependent.

In the 1970s when the symptoms and concept of codependency was first recognized, it described the behaviour patterns of people who were involved in relationships with others who were chemically dependent.

As this field of study expanded it became obvious that the same behaviour patterns were mirrored by those involved with others who engaged in an array of compulsive behaviours, such as eating disorders, as well as gambling and sex addictions.

Co-dependents are people who were raised in families where natural developmental needs were unmet, and where there may have been emotional, mental or physical abuse. Co-dependent and dysfunctional relationships occur from the need people have to feel valued.

The Johnson Institute of Minneapolis, a research institute in the field of addiction, defined codependency as " a set of maladaptive, compulsive behaviours learned by family members to survive in a family experiencing great emotional pain and stress... Behaviours passed on from generation to generation..."

Celebrated author Earnie Larsen describes codependency as "those self-defeating learned behaviours or character defects that result in a diminished capacity to initiate, or participate in, loving relationships".

Author Melody Beattie in her #1 New York Times Bestseller "Codependent No More" calls a co-dependent "... a person who has let someone else's behaviour affect him or her, and is obsessed with controlling other people's behaviour".

Codependency can be many things to different people. In addition to it being about the unhealthy dependent need for other people, it is also about the action or reaction to the moods of others, as well as the behaviours, and expressed thoughts by those same people.

There are two basic types of co-dependent person. The person who is a controller, manipulator, a fixer. I call this type The Aggressor. The other is the person who doesn't seem to know what decisions to make or may be a willing co-conspirator in the subjugation of their own will to that of others and can be a very needy individual. I call this person The Passive. We all have both in us when we are acting out our codependency, however for the sake of illustration I am talking about the dominant character in us, the side of us that is usually present within us most of the time. Depending on the situation or the people involved we would revert to the other character when required. For instance... if I am usually a domineering type of person I may withdraw in the presence of someone who is more domineering. If I am a passive person, I may become a bit more aggressive in the company of someone who is even more passive than I am. In a dysfunctional relationship these two types appear to get along well with one another, and that is usually the case.

Almost everybody wants to control and nobody wants to be controlled. However in real terms there is no such thing as having control over someone. Even though we may think we are controlling a person or that someone has control over us, the answer is a resounding NO!

Why?

We have CHOICES. That's right, choices. Pluto was only discovered in the early part of the 20th century. Astronomers didn't know it was there until 1930. Just because they didn't know it was there doesn't mean it wasn't there. It's been there for a few million years. So, returning to earth and choices... we all have choices. Many of us don't know we have them but we do. Just because we don't know we have them doesn't make them any less existent.

So by extension, this means that control is an illusion. You don't control me. You may think you are controlling me, but you're not. I've made a decision, either consciously or subconsciously, to go along with your advice or suggestion/demand, but I did make that choice. So you haven't controlled me at all.

Simply stated: you can't make me do anything, and I can't make you do anything. Well, the only thing I can make you is lunch. The only person I can control is myself. Accepting this view as reality, allows us to unburden ourselves. We no longer have to try and move the mountain. We no longer have to allow the mountain to try and move us.

Where did this erroneous idea that we can manipulate others come from and why change our behaviour?

It may be considered a paradox that while it is human nature to resist change, it is also a part of who we are to explore new areas, to see what is on the other side of the hill. Throughout human history, people have risked their lives and the lives of others... for what? For the opportunity to provide a better life for themselves and those around them, whether it be scavenging or hunting for bare necessities such as food and water, in locations considered to be dangerous at best and deadly at worst, or perhaps seeking out places that trade in different goods in an effort to introduce a wider variety of products. From climbing the highest mountains, to scouring the densest forests, to sailing beyond the horizon on what was thought to be a flat surface with monsters waiting to devour both the foolish and courageous alike, humans have shown a propensity for change, a devotion to exploration and acquisition.

In concert with the propagation of humans throughout the globe dedicated to discovering that which lay before them, philosophers have for countless centuries opined that the greatest journey is that which takes us within.

This book will deal with issues related to Codependency. It provides a thorough examination of codependency, what it is, where it comes from and how it affects us and our relationships. We will discover what it means to have a healthy, non-dysfunctional relationship with ourself and others. We will explore the paths from which we can choose, and travel along those paths in search of balance, harmony, peace and serenity in all that we do and all that we are.

Addiction

Addiction |ə'dik sh ən|

the fact or condition of being addicted to a particular substance, thing, or activity : ORIGIN late 16th cent. (denoting a person's inclination or proclivity): from Latin addictio(n-), from addicere 'assign'

It is important to note that there are two fundamental characteristics of an addict that define not only what they are, but act as a guiding force in their life that compels them in every thought, emotion and behaviour.

An addict is an extremist. An addict, or to phrase it another way, a person with an addictive personality, will go from one extreme to the other, usually in an instant and without notice. Balance is a foreign land for an addict and if ever aware of it, it is only because they happened to look down and see it there lying somewhere in the middle while travelling from one extreme end of the spectrum to the other. Certainly, they didn't recognize it as anything that looked inviting or even as a real place that could be habitable. A scary and unthinkable place, yet in many cases, a place desired by many people caught in the grips of their dis-ease and vaguely aware that there may be an answer to the constant turmoil of a 'living on the edge' lifestyle manifested in their thoughts, feelings and actions.

The second fundamental characteristic of an addict is that of wanting it all... and wanting it all right NOW! Instant Gratification! This particular trait is increasingly present in modern society with the advent of everything instant.

We have moved from a time where one had to push in a button on the TV and hold it in for the picture to come on the screen. We then went to a TV where the button could be pushed in and released immediately and by the time the viewer crossed the room to sit down the picture was on. Then came remote control, which meant changing channels without getting up from the chair. Now people stand in front of a microwave and with a certain amount of despair in their tone are heard to exclaim, "come on, I haven't got all minute". Living in an 'instant' society is for an addict like throwing petrol on an already blazing flame.

It fuels the fire, increasing expectations and perpetuating the cycle of addiction.

There are two types of addiction: substance and process.

Substance addiction is the type familiar to most people. It is the addiction to substances - that is anything a person can put inside of them self, through inhaling, injection, drinking or eating. It is the alcohol or other drug, and it is the comfort food consumed by millions of people throughout the world. Most addicts will reveal that they take their fix when they are sad or depressed or something is wrong and to mask the feeling of loneliness and rejection. Those very same addicts will also reveal that they take their fix when they are happy or triumphant, as a means to enhance the joyous feeling and use the occasion as an excuse to just use more drugs.

It reminds me of the alcoholic man who told me that there were only two times he ever drank... when he was alone or with someone else! People addicted to a substance will use it to affect their mood while altering their state of mind.

The other type of addiction is that of process. Process addiction encompasses addiction to such things as sex, gambling, Internet, TV, relationships and even the compulsion to wear a green shirt each and every Thursday, to name only a few. It involves a compulsion to act out in ways that do not include substance consumption. However, there is evidence that substantiates the notion that chemical changes occur within the brain during the behaviour to which the person has become addicted. These chemical modifications are similar to those experienced by substance abusers.

It is the understanding and explanation of process addiction which is this book's primary concern and in particular the phenomenon of codependency.

Contrary to what many people have allowed themselves to believe, addiction is not a weakness of character or a glaring lack of willpower. Addiction is a brain disorder and the salient points of this view are detailed in this fine article by Lauran Negroid, which appeared in The Guardian on August 16 2011.

Addiction - A Brain Disorder; Not Just Bad Behaviour

Addiction isn't just about willpower. It's a chronic brain disease, says a new definition aimed at helping families and their doctors better understand the challenges of treating it.

"Addiction is about a lot more than people behaving badly," says Dr. Michael M. Miller of the American Society for Addiction Medicine.

That's true whether it involves drugs and alcohol or gambling and compulsive eating, the doctors group said Monday. And like other chronic conditions such as heart disease or diabetes, treating addiction and preventing relapse is a long-term endeavour, the specialists concluded.

Addiction generally is described by its behavioural symptoms – the highs, the cravings, and the things people will do to achieve one and avoid the other. The new definition doesn't disagree with the standard guide for diagnosis based on those symptoms. But two decades of neuroscience have uncovered how addiction hijacks different parts of the brain, to explain what prompts those behaviours and why they can be so hard to overcome. The society's policy statement, published on its website, isn't a new direction as much as part of an effort to translate those findings to primary care doctors and the general public.

"The behavioural problem is a result of brain dysfunction," agrees Dr. Nora Volkow, director of the National Institute on Drug Abuse.

She welcomed the statement as a way to help her own agency's work to spur more primary care physicians to screen their patients for signs of addiction. NIDA estimates that 23 million Americans need treatment for substance abuse but only about 2 million get that help. Trying to add compassion to the brain findings, NIDA even has made readings from Eugene O'Neill's "Long Day's Journey into Night" a part of meetings where primary care doctors learn about addiction.

Then there's the frustration of relapses, which doctors and families alike need to know are common for a chronic disease, Volkow says.

"You have family members that say, 'OK, you've been to a detox program, how come you're taking drugs?'" she says. "The pathology in the brain persists for years after you've stopped taking the drug."

Just what does happen in the brain? It's a complex interplay of emotional, cognitive and behavioral networks. Genetics plays a role, meaning some people are more vulnerable to an addiction if they, say, experiment with drugs as a teenager or wind up on potent prescription painkillers after an injury.

Age does, too. The frontal cortex helps put the brakes on unhealthy behaviors, Volkow explains. It's where the brain's reasoning side connects to emotion-related areas. It's among the last neural regions to mature, one reason that it's harder for a teenager to withstand peer pressure to experiment with drugs.

Even if you're not biologically vulnerable to begin with, perhaps you try alcohol or drugs to cope with a stressful or painful environment, Volkow says. Whatever the reason, the brain's reward system can change as a chemical named dopamine conditions it to rituals and routines that are linked to getting something you've found pleasurable, whether it's a pack of cigarettes or a few drinks or even overeating. When someone's truly addicted, that warped system keeps them going back even after the brain gets so used to the high that it's no longer pleasurable.

Make no mistake: Patients still must choose to fight back and treat an addiction, stresses Miller, medical director of the Herrington Recovery Center at Rogers Memorial Hospital in Oconomowoc, Wis. But understanding some of the brain reactions at the root of the problem will "hopefully reduce some of the shame about some of these issues, hopefully reduce stigma," he says.

And while most of the neuroscience centers on drug and alcohol addiction, the society notes that it's possible to become addicted to gambling, sex or food although there's no good data on how often that happens. It's time for better study to find out, Miller says.

Meanwhile, Volkow says intriguing research is under way to use those brain findings to develop better treatments — not just to temporarily block an addict's high but to strengthen the underlying brain circuitry to fend off relapse. Topping Miller's wish list: Learning why some people find recovery easier and faster than others, and "what does brain healing look like."

Literature that speaks to addicts seeking relief from their peril contains the following notation: we cannot change the nature of the addict or addiction. We can help to change the old lie "Once an addict, always an addict". It goes on to say: "Addiction is a physical, mental and spiritual disease that affects every area of our lives."

Outlines & Details

At the conclusion of each chapter are certain activities, mostly involving writing. It is suggested that you obtain a note pad and begin to jot down any thoughts or feelings that emerge from topics addressed within these pages. Any behaviours that you feel compelled to engage in can be noted as well. Keep a journal and also use the notepad to compile the words, phrases, sentences and paragraphs resulting from the numbered activity suggestions.

Section I

The Impact

Chapter 1

The Broad Strokes

One of our human traits is the desire to belong. It begins at birth when we develop the need for belonging in order to have our most basic need met; the need for nourishment of two different types - physical nourishment, which is satisfied through consumption of food, and emotional nourishment, which is satisfied through a tactile response of being held or touched.

As we progress through infancy and childhood and realize the fulfillment of our need, we now embody a sense of acceptance and belonging, and feel confident that we are attached to others who care about us and will be our providers. This in turn provides us with a positive sense of self, leading to a sense of positive self-esteem and faith in our own abilities and competency as an individual.

In childhood we would have observed that the type of attention we required and in some instances received - those times being when others listened to us, conversed with us, played with us and validated us - made us feel safe and cared for. We felt we were valued and we belonged.

If we are denied this sense of self, we instead develop fears and a sense of being abandoned. We experience a feeling of being alone and detached from what we need. Often, we begin to fear that we are lacking, we are not good enough and will never experience emotional intimacy. We become despaired, feel depressed and develop further stressful feelings that act out in our thoughts and behaviour. Our natural inclination is to be important to someone, to really matter. We need to know that there is a person who loves us unconditionally. The lack of unconditional love causes stress.

As this stress is not a natural part of our makeup it causes further confusion and causes many people to act out in a manner that would allow us to experience those lost feelings of belonging to something or someone outside of ourselves and subdue or eliminate the negative feelings we experience. Alas, we act out in inappropriate ways that have negative consequences and provide us with a false sense of fulfillment.

*****

When we were neglected we felt emptiness, we felt alone and lonely. To gain a sense that we have merit, that we can belong, to become associated with feelings of pleasure and excitement, we act to fulfill those feelings so as to have the experience NOW! We demand attention, and we engage in activity that will result in the attention we seek. We cry out for someone to provide us with a sense of self and in so doing we harm our self and others.

Being the keen observers we started to become, usually on a subconscious level, we would have experienced the power of those who dismissed us. These powerful people were too busy and too detached to respond to our innocent overtures for need fulfillment, sending us farther and deeper into our world of isolation and despair.

While the response to this behaviour has many permutations, some are singular in nature while others are more common throughout society - One such being that of embodiment of the same traits exhibited by those who failed to nurture us. We attempt to gain power that we can then use to strike back at those who abused us, or power that can be used against others, who are deemed to be weaker and susceptible to manipulation.

As children or adolescents we assert our newfound sense of power only to be overruled with counteraction in the form of more control and punishment. We resist, the countermeasures intensify and the cycle repeats itself. At some point we develop a new strategy in our battle for power and display. That new strategy is often one of disengagement. This type of behaviour serves to alienate us from the very people whose attention we seek and leaves us feeling even more powerless and isolated.

The pain we experience as a result of this profoundly dysfunctional cycle turns to anger, resentment and in many cases fuels retaliation and revenge.

*****

Meanwhile, we have learned that people in authority are not to be trusted or believed. We begin a campaign of lies, cheating and defiance and, in extremes cases, violence and destruction. We feel that those who made us suffer must suffer with us. We construct a persona of will power, strength, competency and confidence. However, at our core, now out of reach because of the fortification that we've constructed, we develop a deep sense of incompetence and inadequacy, coupled with an abiding lack of faith in ourself. We have a sense of hopelessness. We feel that we can never belong.

For people carrying these beliefs and feelings into adulthood, the implications are staggering, leading to ineffective lives, violence in and out of the family, prostitution, sexual, physical, mental and emotional abuse of others, and of children as well as our self.

It needs to be emphasized that the choice of these behaviours which in many instances appears to be premeditated, is at its very depths never made deliberately.

They emerge automatically and unconsciously out of the inner desperate world of pain and loneliness, as the only way we believe will free us and bring us to a place of comfort and a sense of belonging.

It is at this juncture that dysfunctional relationships are formed and people with varying needs either become the willing or unwilling predator or the willing or unwilling victim.

Outlines & Details

1. *Write a paragraph describing the environment in which we felt safe and nurtured. Who were the people that created that environment. Were there objects involved or just people?*

2. *What people and circumstances helped to create a feeling of fear and mistrust? At what time in your life did you become aware of these feelings? Do these feelings still exist?*

Chapter 2

The Core Symptoms

Codependency is a fancy word meaning addiction. The question is always... addiction to what? Answer: addiction to relationships.

Working backwards for a moment... addiction is a dis-ease, and diseases have symptoms. Codependency is a shame-based dis-ease. John Bradshaw, in his critically acclaimed New York Times bestseller Healing The Shame That Binds You writes, "... shame in itself is not bad. Shame is a normal human emotion. It is necessary to have the feeling of shame if one is to be truly human. Shame is the psychological foundation of humility. Toxic shame is unbearable and always necessitates a cover up, a false self. Since one feels his true self is flawed, one needs a false self, which is not defective and flawed."

Let's first explore the symptoms of codependency to better identify any person including our self who may suffer from this dis-ease.

In her groundbreaking book Facing Codependence (Harper Collins), author Pia Mellody sets out the five core symptoms of codependency.

For a powerpoint/slideshow that clearly shows the relationship between the symptoms and the identifying characteristics experienced by people who suffer from this disease go to **http://chesmoulton.com/symptoms**

Core Symptom #1:
Difficulty experiencing appropriate levels of esteem

There are three types of esteem: Low and Superior, which are derived from the messages we receive from others about ourselves, and Other esteem which takes hold of us based on what we feel about ourselves related to the actions of those around us.

Imagine a young girl aged nine. Her parents are visiting her father's work colleague and when it is time to eat, the children are seated at a smaller table of their own, away from the adults who are enjoying their own company at the bigger table. Children, being children, are playing and, being excited the little girl accidentally knocks over her glass of juice which unfortunately spills on the carpet in the dining room. The father comes over to help clean up and scolds the girl unmercifully for her inattention and her inability to control herself. Her father belittles her in front of everyone, even while the host attempts to minimize the impact of the juice on the carpet and explains that it will all come out in the wash.

What is wrong with this picture? The father because of his own esteem issues and the baggage with which he lives condemns his daughter's behaviour because... he may be thinking that the host must wonder if he can't even bring up his child to function properly... that he is a failure at parenthood... he must take responsibility for the girls actions... and any number of other thoughts that could race through his head. When all is said and done, children at the age of nine play and become excited and are not thinking of the carpet or the juice and are still developing their motor skills at the very least. The child was simply doing what children do... she was being a child.

Imagine the impact on the young girl of this scenario played out in different circumstances and repeated over and over as she grows through the years, not to mention the many times it occurred prior to the age of nine.

This child grows up to believe that she is not quite right and she is less than what is expected. She believes that she is unworthy; that she is not able to perform at an acceptable level and perhaps she is not capable of ever being able to please her father. She develops low self-esteem. Her father suffers from Other esteem, as his own sense of worth is tied to the actions of his daughter while imagining whatever dreadful thoughts he has programmed inside of his brain. Oh, and how dare he think for the host, who clearly is not as upset or uncomfortable... even if it is his carpet.

Imagine a boy grows up in a family where he is told that he is better than everyone else in town because his family is prominent and wealthy. He will without much doubt grow into a young man who is dismissive, arrogant and selfish. His level of esteem is unnaturally high

Or perhaps there is a family that never punishes their son and allows him to get away with whatever he wants. He grows into a teenager and when trying to get through and integrate into society, he continues to act out his desires and finds himself not quite getting all that he wanted. As he was never taken to task for misdemeanours at home, he now finds out that while there were no rules inside the family structure, in the world outside there are such things as laws, police, courts and of course jail. Who is responsible in this case? Is it the young boy who did not come to appreciate the rule of law or the parents who let him get away with it all? No matter, the young man clearly suffers from Superior esteem

Core Symptom #2:
Difficulty Setting Functional Boundaries

In our formative years, as a consequence of being the unwanted participant of dysfunctional circumstances, we develop a need for attachment with another individual for the purpose of survival. We lack the belief that we are capable and may even experience feelings of alienation leading to isolation. We feel unacceptable and unaccepted. As a consequence of these feelings we build walls that keep us safe from others, safe from those who hurt us by rejecting us as well as those who trespass onto us. No one gets in and we don't go out!

Many people go through life surrounded by emotional walls. These walls have been constructed to keep others from getting in too close, or in fact getting in at all, while other walls are built as a means of keeping that same person from getting out and experiencing the world and the people who inhabit it.

These walls are erected because the person has a fear. Many people fear incorrectly, that they lack the interpersonal skills, the emotional aptitude as well as the mental strength to properly or successfully interact with others. They not only have a fear based on what often is an incorrect assumption of their own abilities, they are also afraid of any emotional upheaval occurring that may cause them to experience many of the emotions that are a usual part of living in a world that is inhabited by every kind of person imaginable. Walls keep people on the outside from getting in and keep the person on the inside from coming out.

Moreover, many people who live their life behind walls exhibit an anger, the root of which is buried deep inside and grown out of a mistrust of others. In many instances the anger is centred around the frustration of not being able to have the life they would desire, due to their inability to trust, which they blame on others.

Many people who have erected walls and live an angry life build in a defense mechanism that basically will reject others before they themself feel rejected, whether that rejection is real or imagined, in that they don't give others a chance to accept them for who they are and the contribution they can make.

Boundaries, on the other hand, are permeable walls that with the implementation of certain criteria can provide a safe and secure system with which to experience the world in which we live and all the people with whom we come in contact. Think in terms of a boundary between country A and Country B. Imagine that boundary marking the area that denotes where country A ends and country B begins... or vice versa. Whether you see the boundary as a beginning or an ending depends on your viewpoint and how you understand the world around you.

Now take that image of the boundaries and transpose it into emotional, mental and behavioural functions. Many people who are codependent remain unaware that they can knock down the walls that surround them and build a set of boundaries that will provide for a more fruitful and enjoyable life.

Other people who are also codependent have no boundaries whatsoever and no sense of respect for other people's boundaries - or in fact others people's walls - and will trespass with no apologies, for the purposes that suit them. The trespasser is also operating from a fear-based position, and it is this type of person who terrifies others into rejecting any suggestion that they deconstruct their own walls and instead build boundaries. While it does take effort to maintain and guard one's boundaries, the effort exerted is far less than that required to maintain and refortify a construction of walls.

Further, there are many instances of people who do not exhibit any walls and seemingly have no boundaries who are not the offensive type previously described. They are instead people who are unhappily the victims. While most of these people without proper guidance will live their lives being a perpetual victim, some will reach a point where they lash out and become the victimizer. These new victimizers, while possibly taking aim at their own former abusers and others who are unfortunate to cross their path, perpetuate another characteristic of a codependent person or in other words a person with an addictive personality, in that they have now gone to the other extreme.

Core Symptom #3:
Difficulty owning our own reality.

Given the abundance of confusing emotional, mental and behavioural disorders acted out by people in a society, it is little wonder that many people are unable to accept responsibility for the role they play in acting out in their world and have difficulty in knowing who they are and how to properly experience their life. Not only can people be generally unaware of their place in a larger environment, they can also be oblivious to their own personal reality. Humans only do three things. We think. We feel. We act. For the purpose of considering our own reality we must add another element, the physical.

Codependents become seized with the following issues and lack appropriate mechanisms to deal with the basics of life.

Thinking:	How we interpret the world that surrounds us as well as our own thoughts, and how we output this data.
Feeling:	Inability to get in touch with our feelings or, once in touch, suffer an overwhelming emotive response.
Behaviour:	Inability to determine a proper course of action, which may also mean taking no action, and being unaware of the impact or consequences of our action or inaction.

Physical: Being unaware or in denial of our bodies with respect to how they function and appear to our self as well as others.

Difficulty in owning one's own reality can be looked at from two very different perspectives. Some people who exhibit this trait do so from pure ignorance and denial of who they are and the effects of that denial on those around them - as well as the affect it may have on their self if they were to acknowledge their reality. Others who struggle with owning and accepting their reality do so out of fear - fear of being exposed and, additionally, fear of being rejected.

Core Symptom #4:
Difficulty acknowledging and meeting our own needs and wants.

Each person has needs, some of which can only be fulfilled by the individual. The core needs that a person usually seeks to have satisfied are those involving food, shelter, medical attention, clothing, physical, emotional and mental nurturing, as well as financial stability.

Fulfillment of other needs and wants require interaction with other people.

Many people become confused and are unable to distinguish between what is needed and what they want. They have some recourse to their wants, and therefore are unaccustomed to the experience of having their needs fulfilled. Alternately they are aware of their needs and wants but neglect to seek out others to assist in fulfillment, and as a result, usually go without.

It is the people who populate this category who often act out inappropriately by abusing themselves in an attempt to either mask the anger, fear, and loneliness, caused by the confusion.

Others remain totally unaware of their needs as well as their wants and many are convinced they have no needs and wants. This trait in adults can be traced to a time in their formative years when they experienced constant neglect from their caregivers. Ultimately, they arrive as adults and seek to please others in a vain hope that the individuals on whom they bestow their attention will mirror their selfless actions and thoughts.

Furthermore, there are people who become totally dependent on others to supply their needs and wants, either from a position of dominance, in that they expect to be cared for, and those who require others to meet their needs because they do not know how to care for themself.

Conversely we must also become aware that we may be required to meet the needs of others at appropriate times and under proper circumstances.

The lack of need fulfillment is just one more example of an inappropriate level of self-esteem.

Core Symptom #5:
Difficulty experiencing and expressing our reality moderately.

Having already noted that a codependent has an addictive personality and exhibits behaviour, thoughts and feelings that reside on one end of the spectrum or the other, it is easy to imagine a person who cannot express their self in a moderate form or fashion.

Harking back to the core symptom of not taking responsibility for our own reality, it is easy to understand the symptoms that play out in this area of codependency.

The extremist will be a person who either dresses to expose their body inappropriately to gain as much attention as possible or will be one who dresses to hide as much of their body, its shape, its contours and its size in the hope of becoming invisible and non-existent.

Many people display an all-or-nothing extremist approach to thinking. People who are codependent think in terms of black or white, up or down, left or right, hot or cold, good or bad, wrong or right. There is no middle ground for these people and to suggest they attempt to see something that for them does not exist (and if it did would be useless), is to invite rancour, dissent, disrespect and suspicion. Their thinking revolves around a simple premise that you are either with them or against them.

The realm of expressive emotions or the total lack of emotional response is another hallmark of a codependent. While the absence of emotional output may be evident, this person may have one of two extremes within. This person does experience internal feelings while choosing not to express them or is unable to express them or has no feelings of which they are aware. The other type of person, one who is very cognizant of their feelings, is that person who is extroverted, exuberant, and seemingly oblivious to the impact their outrageous expression may have on their immediate environment.

Outlines & Details

1. *What are your symptoms of codependency? Have they impacted your life in a positive or negative manner, or both? How?*

2. *If you have an inappropriate level of esteem, what could you do to help yourself attain the level you want?*

3. *Are you in touch with your feelings? Are you able to express them safely and confidently?*

4. *Can you identify your actions and thoughts that are connected to certain feelings?*

Chapter 3

How To Become Codependent

The road to becoming codependent is a short one, and no one becomes codependent on their own. Codependency being a dis-ease concentrated on dysfunctional relationships is concerned with learned type behaviours. These behaviours are learned during our childhood. We learn to be dysfunctional at a very young age, soon after we are born.

Codependency is a dis-ease of the developing self whereby a child's natural need for nurturing and guidance is unrealised.

Self-actualization, a term first coined by organizational theorist Kurt Goldstein, was later adopted by developmental psychologist Abraham Maslow. Maslow advanced the notion that the needs of humans could be categorized and slotted into a hierarchy with basic needs being the first category of needs-fulfillment.

Maslow further proposed that each need coincided with an action required to relieve the person of that need. The required action was either provided by another person or group of people or was in concert with the actions of the person expressing the need.

For the healthy development of an individual to be manifested, it is vital that the need being expressed be fulfilled during the timeframe in which the person is experiencing the particular need.

A baby expressing a need for food, or some other basic needs, such as physical comfort from having a dry diaper or the feeling that comes from being held, will experience the need as normal stress. The caregiver will be alerted to this stress/need because the baby is crying.

The baby will experience this stress/need for a time that is unique to that infant. Many caregivers, acting on misguided intention, will allow the baby to continue to "cry it out" thinking it is not only good for the infant's lungs but will teach the newborn or young child that they cannot or will not be able to have their own way whenever they demand it. The baby now deprived of its needs, increases the crying to further emphasize the need being deprived.

The level of normal stress experienced by the baby increases to a level of distress which then becomes painful. When the child experiences repeated deprivation of its needs it will turn off the need so as to avoid the pain associated with the deprivation.

While the caregiver may be led to believe that the baby has altered its behaviour in an understanding that it is unable to control the adult, it has in fact learned that people cannot be trusted or depended upon for whatever is required for relief of their needs.

Pain and dysfunction become automatic responses as a child experiences mind alteration in an effort to suppress emotions. As we get older we forget because the trauma was so devastating the memories become repressed and anxiety remains unexpressed, causing us to act out or act in with inappropriate behaviour that contaminates our lives and the lives of others.

When this cycle is repeated throughout a child's formative years, the child disengages from the need experience and instead experiences internal emotional and mental confusion.

It doesn't end there!

As children get older and even in adulthood, the cycle, upon being repeated, will continue to negatively affect a person's emotional maturity and impact on how they view the world, affect their own self-worth and at the same time contribute to the development of tension within the physical plane of the individual that resides with varying degrees of intensity. This tension locates itself in the muscular, skeletal and gastro - intestinal systems as well as others.

The critical nature of these tensions, which demand attention and relief, compel the individual to construct a "Want" system, which is very different than our "Need" system. "Wants" over a very short period of time become constant and extensive while demanding relief; whereas "needs" once satisfied can induce comfort and relaxation for extended periods of time.

Interaction with our "want system" teaches us to choose substances and behaviours as a means of gaining relief from tensions.

A child, shunned from a group of others and feeling rejected complains to a caregiver and is given a treat and told that it will help in making that child feel better. Repeated experience of this behaviour will teach the child that food will take away unhappy or sad feelings.

Fast forward to the years when a young person is induced by others to adopt the idea that consuming alcohol will eliminate fears; fear of engagement with others for the purpose of companionship and the possible rejection from seeking intimacy; fear of authority figures; fear of failure related to promotion at work or career advancement; fear of public speaking... and the list goes on. This individual learns that alcohol eliminates fear.

Consumption of substances or the adoption of certain behaviours in an effort to relieve inner tension and turmoil becomes a learned behaviour set to repeat itself throughout adult living experiences. Simply stated... we feel bad... we find something that makes us feel good... no one wants to feel bad... so we engage in behaviour that makes us feel good, and we do it over and over and over again. We engage in symptomatic behaviour instead of addressing the cause of the tensions and the associated behaviour.

A woman age 40 years has each morning of her adult life awoken with her left hand entangled in her hair. From the age of four to fifteen, her drunken father would sexually abuse her and during each episode she realized that if she laid perfectly still and rigid while slowly pulling her hair by the roots, the unbearable pain she inflicted upon herself separated her from the overwhelming and severe reality of the abuse she received from her father. Her mind said: "This is not happening", while her feelings became numb, empty, frozen. She concentrated on the pain of pulling her hair to maintain survival.

These are people who choose or are taught not to feel, as a means of disengaging from their negative feelings, such as fear, anger and shame, because of abuse they are suffering with no means of escape.

This distortion through the development of the "want system" away from the authentic human experience of one's own needs leads to a distortion of the meaning and intentions of people and events, and a distortion of the perceptions of and the meaning ascribed to others' intentions and behaviors as well as our own.

It is true to say that most people are unaware of the deeper tension inside of themselves or the originating cause of that tension and are merely acting out on what they believe is a bad feeling existing on the surface or distress caused by a series of events. There is another group of affected people who have a sense that all is not well and may desire to investigate the origins of their unwanted behaviour, and a third group who, while aware that their behaviour is undesirable, do not seek to modify it.

The messages we receive as well as some we do not, contribute to our sense of self. Many messages are direct and overt, while other messages are more subliminal and covert. It is true that while some messages that are direct do not register as being an idea or notion that once adopted could negatively impact our behaviour, it must be realized that children do not concern themselves with the impactful nature of content... they are children!

Notwithstanding as already outlined that some in society have developed an inappropriate level of esteem that allows for a misguided sense of superiority, most people who suffer from an inappropriate level of esteem, suffer from low self esteem.

Many people have reported that one of the messages they received while growing up was that if they thought too much of themselves they were considered conceited and this behavioural output was condemned - they were teased in the schoolyard, and shunned by fellow classmates and playmates.

We were taught as a whole that we were not to look inward. Our attention must be on what is around us and outside of ourselves. We were taught to put everyone else first and ourself last. It was implied that we were selfish, rude and insubordinate to imagine that we could amount to more than we were allowed. We were conditioned to put our focus on those around us, be secondary to them in a selfless quest to serve and be seen or known to be polite and congenial in an ordered society. Whether that society consisted of the people in a confined family, neighbourhood, or a larger community.

As a consequence of learning to deflect attention from ourself we completely abandon any sense of worth and look to others to inform us of our value.

Having established that codependency is a process addiction, people who exhibit any of the attendant character traits can be identified as having an addictive personality. The evidence indicates that these traits are developed in childhood. While one can be born with a neurobiological makeup that destines that person to being an addict... the follow on question being whether they are a practicing addict or not, and if so to what degree... much of the dysfunctional traits exhibited in a codependent person are learned behaviours.

Many of these traits become ingrained in the codependent from or for a variety of influences and reasons. Many children consciously and subconsciously adopt certain behaviour patterns as they grow in age as well as experience in an effort to mimic behaviour exhibited by a parent or caregiver. These patterns can be used as a mechanism for survival while being either aggressive or passive in nature.

Contained in his inspirational book titled Stage II Recovery-Life Beyond Addiction (Harper & Row), author Earnie Larsen sets out an explicit discourse on self-defeating learned behaviours and offers a rather detailed but not exhaustive explanation, of six personality types, identified as being the result of emersion in a dysfunctional environment.

A brief synopsis established by Mr. Larsen, of these character types can be found at: http://chesmoulton.com/behaviors

Additionally, community and religious leaders, educational authorities and media contribute to the messages received by the population in a society. Young people, while in their formative years, in the absence of contradiction are apt to absorb and believe messages received from authority figures and institutions, some examples of which follow.

For decades the radio airwaves have filled our minds with images and beliefs that others are responsible for our emotions and have informed us of what is the correct mental posture to adopt. An entertainer, popular in the 1950's and 60's, once sang lyrics informing listeners "you're nobody until somebody loves you". The context in which this statement was made, related to a love relationship between two consenters and not to a parental-child bond. So, if I am not romantically involved in a relationship... I'm nobody... I'm worthless. Seems a bit trite this argument, but consider that this message and hundreds more on a daily basis are blasted over the airwaves. The messages while consciously believed by perhaps not the entire listening public, do impact subconsciously on the image they have of themselves.

This alone is not enough to chronically damage one's perception of self and create a standard of behaviour that is deemed to be deeply codependent; however, it is only one area of messaging that informs a person. Added to this is the fact that the purveyor of this information... the singer... is hugely popular and very many impressionable people will be swayed by the argument contained in the lyrics. For many years I thought that this was the worst example of dysfunctional thinking. Then one day, while driving along, I tuned into a radio station to hear the following lyric which - to this day - remains tied for first place with the earlier articulation. The lyric is "I'd rather have bad times with you than good times with someone else". The name of the performer remains to me a mystery. This is the height of dysfunctional self-loathing thinking and behaviour. Traditional popular music for decades has erroneously taught us to believe that others are responsible for our feelings. Lyrics such as... "if you leave me I will die"... "I can't live without you"... "you make me sad"... you make me mad"... "you make me happy" all contribute to perpetuate the notion that it is not inside of me, but outside of me. In the absence of authority speaking out against the nature of these messages, (and how could they, in their ignorance, not knowing at that time in cultural history the nature or impact of these words) people will go merrily along their way, embracing songs the lyrics of which speak to their situation at that present moment. Moreover, in the absence of authority explaining the impact these lyrics, the general population remains oblivious and consigns their immediate thinking to the notion that... there can be nothing wrong with a song that tells me how to feel and who is responsible. If there was something wrong about this, it would not have been allowed on the radio or there would at least be people rallying against it.

This is not to be confused with objection raised by many conservative thinkers during the 1960's and 70's to the sexually explicit nature and lyrics of many performers and entertainers

Imagine a young girl around the age of six or seven. Her mother tucks her into bed each night with part of the ritual being the recitation of the following prayer: Now I lay me down to sleep, I pray the Lord my soul to keep. If I should die before I wake, I pray the Lord my soul to take. While I fully understand the significance behind the words in the prayer, one must note that the child has an active subconscious mind that adopts the belief that it is entirely possible that she will die in her sleep and not see her family, friends, etc., ever again. Now while it is possible this could very well happen, it is not probable. Yet, it conjures up images of death and abandonment in a young child, who is concerned with nothing else but praying to the God in whom she is being taught to believe.

As children, we are bombarded with so many messages, so often, and usually with no explanation from 'responsible' adults. The messages are confusing and whether premeditated or accidental - inform, influence and challenge us while purporting to assist us in our learning curve of how we interpret and act, or react, to our immediate environment, both internal and external. We take much for granted and when confusing ideas are presented, we become confused as to which direction we will go and with whom.

A young boy, while growing up is never told that he has any good ideas. While not berated or belittled, he is ignored by his parents and is not validated. His father is a bit of a controller and is essentially unresponsive to the emotional needs that the boy requires as a natural part of becoming aware of himself and his environment and growth.

The boy grows into manhood.

There is a young woman who is weak and ineffectual. She seemingly does not possess the ability to make decisions. Each weekday morning she stands in front of her open closet and struggles to know what clothes to wear to her workplace. She suffers from paralysis of analysis.

The young man who was not validated and the indecisive young lady are a match made in heaven for all the wrong reasons. He has grown up to become a controller, much like his father. He is assertive, if not at times aggressive in nature and likes to tell people how to run their lives. She, on the other hand, is unsure of herself and afraid of being wrong.

He thrives on being able to help her sort out her clothes, advise her where she ought to live and even pick her friends for her.

He does all this not necessarily because he has an emotional attachment. Well, he does actually, but it is not a healthy love relationship. He wants to get that pat on the back. He wants her, and others, to tell him he is smart and has good ideas, and makes good decisions. He is getting his self-esteem, not from within himself... but from her and others. He depends on them to make him feel good about himself.

She on the other hand tells herself: "Well I can't be all that bad. This big decisive, powerful, wonderful man wouldn't waste his time on me if I was just a nothing type of person. He would not be attracted to me if I were really an awful and weak person. He wouldn't take time out of his life to come over here and look after me if I was nobody. I can't be that bad after all." And she says it all with a reassuring smile.

She has her validation needs met from outside of herself and he gets his needs met through her. They are subconsciously using each other to raise their personal level of esteem.

This relationship could carry on indefinitely, or it may last only as long as it takes our hero to find new minds to conquer.

Where did this erroneous idea, that we can manipulate others, come from? How about some ideas that have been with us a lifetime, such as "you can make it happen", "you gotta get in there and make it work"?.

If these clichés were meant to empower us, it is my contention that they missed the mark by a wide margin. I propose another well worn but often neglected cliché- Live And Let Live. I'll allow you to do what you need to do for yourself and you allow me to live my life the best way I can. If I make suggestions to you on how I think you may do it different, I know that at the end of the day you will choose (there's that word again) to do what you believe suits you best. You may choose to accept my advice in whole or in part, perhaps modifying it to suit, or you may simply choose to reject it totally. That's your choice and I'll accept that.

A difficult thing to do because it involves letting go! Especially difficult when the person is someone we care about. However, we must not rob them of a chance to learn from their experiences. At the very least, it will allow them to improve their ability to make choices that are positive, and at the most we learn to respect other people's right to choose. We may gain their respect in so doing.

As defined in the opening pages, addiction is a pathological relationship to a substance or process regardless of the consequences. Whenever a body-mind-spirit-emotion become devalued by one process or another, the process can then be classed as a disease and can remain so even in the face of adverse consequences.

The British rock band Supertramp described the situation quite accurately in their song titled The Logical Song. The lyrics imply that as children we are taught one thing and a very different set of expectations are presented at some point after, only adding to the confusion already being experienced by the child or adolescent.

When I was young, it seemed that life was so wonderful, a miracle, it was beautiful, magical

And all the birds in the trees, well they'd be singing so happily, joyfully, playfully, watching me

But then they send me away to teach me how to be sensible, logical, responsible, practical

And they showed me a world where I could be so dependable, clinical, intellectual, cynical

There are times when all the world's asleep
The questions run too deep for such a simple man
Won't you please, please tell me what we've learned
I know it sounds absurd but please tell me who I am

I said now, watch what you say, now we're calling you a radical, a liberal, fanatical, criminal

Won't you sign up your name, we'd like to feel you're acceptable, respectable, presentable, a vegetable

But at night, when all the world's asleep
The questions run so deep for such a simple man
Won't you please (Won't you tell me), (You can tell me what) please tell me what we've learned (Can you hear me?)
I know it sounds absurd, (Won't you help me) please tell me who I am, who I am, who I am, who I am

But I'm thinking so logical
Did you call, one two three four
It's getting unbelievable

Songwriters: Richard Davies, Roger Hodgson
The Logical Song lyrics © Universal Music Publishing Group

Outlines & Details

1. *Who are the people in your life that seem to trigger your codependency?*

2. *What are the circumstances?*

3. *What are some ways you can start taking care of yourself ?*

Chapter 4

The Family System

A family environment can be healthy, creative, progressive. In healthy families, children grow up and move into another family system. They become autonomous. People who possess a healthy self-image will be drawn to people who share the same attributes of thinking, feeling and behaviour. They will reject overtures to become involved in unhealthy and dysfunctional relationships.

In a dysfunctional family system people remain immature; power struggles develop, issues related to unresolved pain are created and sustained. People can feel as if they are being held hostage, and are made to believe that they are stupid or crazy. This scenario is based on a mistaken belief system. Children are often taught to not to think, not to talk and not to feel. Two basic human needs are missing: trust and openness.

What passes as "normal" parenting in society is in large measure, abusive. "Normal" parenting denies the child the opportunity to discover who they really are, as they are instructed to suppress their emotions and offer unwavering obedience. Many children become further damaged because their adult caregivers seek to have their own inner child needs met from the very child to whose care they have been entrusted. The wounded child who grows into a dysfunctional adult suffering from their own loss of nurturing is responsible for much of the pain and dysfunction that exists in the world.

Dysfunctional families have hidden secrets that often go back three or four generations. They hide their own truths and act out distorted thinking patterns that lead to control and perfectionism. Traits include but are not limited to, rigid and inflexible rules and beliefs i.e.: "my way or the highway!"

Alternatively, because addiction is a dis-ease of extremes, we are just as likely to internalize the worst parts of our parents and caregivers, under the mantra of doing to ourselves what was done to us.

Addictive behaviour, acting out, or in many cases directing the dysfunctional behavior inside of our self, known as self defeating behaviour, is extreme. We do to our self and others what was done to us... or the exact opposite.

Extremist behaviour manifests by way of going all out or not going at all. Some people trust everyone while others trust no one. Some people are extreme extroverts while others hesitate to reply when spoken too.

It has been said that emotions are the mind's mirror into the soul. Emotionally stuck people cannot experience their own reality much less express their reality. Reality is lost, not embraced.

In a dysfunctional family system what the parents say does not correspond with their actions. Take a very common example acted out between a mother and child, which - on the face of it - seems so innocent. The mother for any number of reasons finds herself, bent over sitting in a chair, alone in a room, crying. The young child walks into the room and asks what is the matter, what is wrong. The mother responds that there is nothing wrong, and dismisses the child. Clearly, there is something wrong or the mother would not be crying. While I'm not suggesting that that mother be obliged to disclose what most probably is an adult situation, she could consider reassuring the child that while all is not usual it is not the child's fault that she is crying and to console the child from any sad/bad emotions resulting from the episode.

Children live in a magical world where everything is expanded, resulting in expanded pain, which in turn blocks or skewers reality. False beliefs about oneself become ingrained.

A little girl, lacking validation through her mother about her father, will later in life gravitate toward males to "fix" her. A boy who is not given a sense of female feelings and thinking by his father will enter into relationships with women to be "fixed". The unsuspecting partner quickly finds himself/herself in a "reactionship" or "hostage situation", not knowing how to respond.

Individuals who become involved with practicing addicts are people who are hurting inside and perform self-defeating behaviours due to accumulated emotional pain, such as projected anger and guilt. This pain began for most people during their childhood and carries over into future relationships. These behaviours become ingrained throughout the individual's life and result in personality disorders such as compulsions, post traumatic stress disorders, anxiety, panic attacks and phobias.

Codependents are people in a relationship with abusers. Codependents are tormented by other people's behaviour. To the addict, they are a necessary nuisance. They are controlling, manipulative, difficult to communicate with, at times become downright hateful and a hindrance to the addict getting their "fix". If the addict is a substance abuser, the codependent may pour alcohol down the sink, throw out drugs and become the household police in an effort to keep the addict from getting "high". They remain loyal and continue to rescue the addict from their disasters. They do not understand the addict and are known to say things like "if you love me, you'll stop using" or "how could you do this to the children".

Many codependents while appearing strong on the outside and projecting an aura of being in control and masterful, are themselves weak inside and often fearful of people discovering the truth. Many people use this false bravado to camouflage what they believe is their true nature.

Apart from general patterns that identify a person as codependent, each person is unique and each situation is complex.

Some people have extremely difficult and painful experiences with codependency, while others may be only mildly affected. Each person has a unique makeup of codependent issues evolving from their situation, history and personality.

The common denominator running through the life of a codependent involves relationships with other people, who may be alcoholics, gamblers, sex addicts, workaholics - to name only a few. Codependency involves the effects these people have on the codependent and the manner in which they in turn attempt to affect those individuals.

A codependent is one who becomes affected by the actions of another person and in turn becomes obsessed with controlling that person's behaviour. Codependency involves a habitual system of thinking, feeling and behaviour towards oneself and others that causes emotional and mental stress.

While codependency is acted out in various behavioural patterns, such as workaholism or pursuit of perfectionism, there are two main themes consistent in most people suffering from this dis-ease. Many people are caretakers while many others are people pleasers.

People Pleaser

Many adults who have experienced neglect by their caregivers, rather than lashing out and becoming spiteful, will become docile, needy and compliant in order to obtain the love and acceptance denied them in their youth. Moreover, they are instilled with the belief that their neediness is further evidence of their weakness and improper behaviour. In an effort to receive the love and validation they require, they expose themselves to abuse by others, who are willing to use them for whatever nefarious means will suit their own dysfunctional needs. They become people pleasers.

There are two types of people pleasers. One type is a person who volunteers to be used by others in an effort to fit in and become accepted as a person who is willing to "do what it takes". In almost every instance this person is never accepted. The actions evoked by their insatiable need to please is what they see as their way in. Those who use them, sense their hunger and deem it to be the weakness; it is much like the cravings of a substance abuser for a fix. This people pleaser continues to offer and others continue to take and abuse the person, by using them and never giving them the reward they seek.

The other type of people pleaser is a person who allows others to walk all over them. This person is a doormat. While they may not make a concerted effort to offer to do the biding of others in an attempt to please and gain favour, they cannot and will not say "no" to others who trespass over their boundary. They are under the impression that if they say no, the other person will not like them and will speak and think badly about them.

People pleasers see it as their duty to do the bidding of others, whether they seek out that relationship or it comes knocking on the door. This incessant need is tied directly to their own sense of self. The amount of inconvenience, use and abuse they endure is limitless. It is in very many instances, fatal.

Caretaker

The other, more frequent personality type that acts out from the lack of having their needs met, is that of Caretaker. A caretaker is someone who needs to be loved, but not for obeying others or trying to please people.

Caretakers base their self image on how much they can do for others. They see their main task in life as that of looking after others and, as a result, never learn to take care of themselves. Caretakers seek out dependent people. The codependent person seeking to "fix" people exerts tremendous effort, many times in the face of great odds, with the singular - usually subconscious - thought, that fixing this person will make up for not being able to help the misguided parent or older sibling or relative. Another caretaker scenario is one where the caretaker wants to act, think and emote better than they were able to previously, with the hope that the surrogate parent will now provide them with whatever it was they missed on the way to not having their developmental needs fulfilled.

Caretakers are those people who have little or no respect for other peoples boundaries and usually have nonexistent boundaries for themselves. They see it as their duty and goal in life to look after other people, showering them with ideas and bombarding them with the amount of attention that borders on - and in many cases typifies - emotional, mental and physical trespassing. They act out their need for closeness, validation, and attention by "always being there" for others. Often the caretaking codependent becomes enmeshed with those from whom they seek validation. When a person receives their identity or sense of self from another, that person is enmeshed and codependent. Phrases like "I'll die without you" and "without you I'm nothing" are the common themes of caretakers.

Many years ago while explaining the concept and perils of being a caretaker to a client who was seeking relief from the turmoil caused by her unmanageable behaviour, I was able to assist her in feeling comfortable about the "letting go" stage. It is paramount to moving away from this crippling mindset. In so doing, I urged her to consider using the following phrase when explaining her new intentions to those with whom she had engaged: "I still care about you, but I can no longer care for you" She reported that in some cases there was almost a gnashing of teeth as some of the people to whom she had become attached were themselves codependent and were in desperate need to have someone look after them and run their lives. In other cases there was a collective sigh of relief, from people who had resented the constant intrusion and attempts at control, but were perhaps to polite to say anything for fear of being thought rude or offending. These same people were themselves suffering from a mild form of codependency; in that they suffered unnecessarily because they lacked the fortitude to politely, but firmly, establish a boundary with the caretaking individual.

Many people mistake abuse for love, because it was what they received when they were young. They could not imagine that their caregivers would not show them love and attention in a nurturing manner, so they believed that what they received was love. As adults, they choose abuse and continue to stay in an abusive environment because they believe it is love.

Think for a moment of a person who is involved with an abusive partner. The relationship quickly deteriorates and it make no logical sense for that abused person to continue in the relationship. However, the premise for which the abused person continues in the relationship is not contained in logic. It is an emotional link that keeps the person in a dysfunctional setting. Both parties are playing out their own need for validation. The abuser often is the person who is lashing out, literally, to gain some sense of control, from within, while at the same time seeking to gain merit from those whom he abuses.

At best the abuser wants to be lauded and at worst is so self centred, not caring for the wilful admiration of others and only concerned with the conflict raging inside, oblivious to or uncaring of, the pain inflicted on others.

The child and ego states are once again working in concert in delivering the message that the abuser is unworthy of love and appreciation. The abuser subconsciously selects - or is selected - by a person seeking validation. The cycle begins whereby the abuser must control the other into submission in a vain attempt to prove to the voices inside that they have achieved that which was denied.

An adult woman endlessly taking care of others and resenting it. Codependents see it as their duty to worry about other people and their problems. They call their behaviour kindness, love, and sometimes righteous indignation. Caretakers are "other focused" and often murmur "why is he doing this to me?"

The abused person remains in the relationship, in order to prove that they can maintain a relationship and further prove that they can move mountains, by willing the abuser to modify behaviour. In some instances, the abused person's child ego state will tell them that it is their own fault that they are being abused and they will seek to blame their own self for the actions of their partner. They will become convinced that the continued abuse is evidence that their own change in behaviour is still not good enough to please their abusive partner. They will continue to look for ways in which they can change to please the abuser, never knowing that it is not about them. It is about the abuser!

Alternately, people remain in an abusive and unloving relationship out of fear - not necessarily due to fear of their partner, but due to fear of being alone.

The thinking is that if the person leaves them, or if they initiate the breakup they may never get "love" in their life. Their fears are based on their own personal history that tells them that they had not had love prior to meeting this person. So they become fearful that they will never find love again. They feel they are worthless and very lucky that someone has taken an interest in them. As we have learned previously, the other partner is "loving" them for who they are..a person lacking self esteem to the point that they are willing to become submissive in an attempt to please their partner and receive the real love they so desperately crave, or, they are a person who confuses abuse for love and experiences brief episodes of affection, which only makes the abuse worth it even more.

The extreme behaviour by both partners, exemplifies their addictive personality in that the abuser swings from abuse to love, while the victim tolerates the abuse due to the misguided thinking that it is normal to have such wide swings and that the more conflict there is within the relationship, the more love there must be as well. Clearly, the victim is seeking the love they were denied as a child growing up in a dysfunctional family system.

Couples who are caught up in a negative cycle of fight and flirt, are another example of the dysfunction playing out in many relationships. The scenario is that they both have witnessed this type of activity among adults when they were still in their formative years. Believing that it is perfectly natural to sustain conflict and argument in a relationship, they come to expect it. In many cases, they will prove dissent in order to maintain that which is familiar, and as a means to building up to the release of intimacy (there's the "love"...) to reinforce the notion that not only are they loved and in the right relationship, also that they are valued and have merit.

Hence a reminder of the lyrics previously mentioned..."I'd rather have bad times with you, than good times with someone else". This person has confused pain for passion. Similarly, to the pattern that was experienced in childhood, negative abusive attention is better than no attention at all.

There is a contrast between a person who does move from one abusive relationship to another, wondering why they always end up with the same type of partner, no matter how determined they are not to repeat the mistakes of the past - and - a person who maintains an abusive relationship full in the believe that it is love and there is not another who would love them like this. Unfortunately..there are plenty!

Outlines & Details

1. Is there a person or situation in your life that you are trying to control? Why?

2. What are the benefits to you of this controlling behaviour?

3. How is the other person benefiting by your attempts to control?

4. What would happen to you if you stopped trying to control the situation or person?

Section II

The Evidence

Chapter 5

The Inner Child and Its Relations

The ego state is the psyche in totality. It is the sum of all components that converge to make us who we are, for better or for worse.

In our attempt to understand and explain why we think, feel and act in certain ways at certain times with certain people, we can examine ourselves from another point of reference having to do with some parts of our psychological makeup. Our psyche is constructed of several parts that influence us depending on circumstances and the stimulation involved. Many aspects of our psyche remain hidden in our subconscious, and are a result of the treatment we received as infants and children. Our subconscious is a repository of most of our lives' events and its memory banks store just about everything that we have experienced through all of our five senses. We think, feel and act out based on the associations we have with events from the past that are stored in our subconscious as well as the associations we have that may be related to our wishes and expectations for future events. Triggers that are related to the thoughts, feelings and behaviours can be emotional, mental and physical. Visual, audio and tactile triggers may also impact on how we think, act and feel in relation to past events. Other aspects of who we are were developed in our adult life and remain in our conscious awareness.

Humans and trees have something in common. If you examine the inner trunk of a tree, you will see the core of that tree, which represents what the tree was. That inner core is the younger tree, still living within the physically matured tree. Within each adult human is the essence of who they were... a child. A term known as "inner child" became a part of our language to identify and describe the core essence of our being. For many people, that inner child remains an active part of who they are as an adult.

It is the child personality within us that demands instant gratification. The child personality is immature, underdeveloped and needy. Lending itself to narcissistic tendencies, selfish and impulsive behaviour, the child personality has the potential to commit the most harm, while binding the adult in chains to a life of acting out in an effort to get what it wants and have it NOW!

Often, many people have more than one manifestation of their inner child living within and acting out as they navigate their way through life. An example of this can be demonstrated through the explanation of a story about a client who, at that time was in his early thirties. Through some very intensive inner exploration and hard work, he was able to determine two manifestations of his little self. One was a boy that was himself at or around the age of seven, while the other was identified as being that same man, but stuck around the ages of fifteen or seventeen.

It is my contention that the ages in which we are represented by our younger selves has to do with events in our childhood and youth, that would have stunted us emotionally. As we continue to grow, both physically and mentally we a leave part of us behind that does not grow with us as we mature, but rather stays stuck at the point where trauma had impacted and served to limit the wholeness that until that point we might have enjoyed.

As an adult it is interesting to witness when various parts that make us who we are exhibit themselves for others to see. What is the stimuli that evokes the little boy in my client to come out and be on parade? What is happening at the time the teenager within the adult decides it is his turn to take over and act out? How are these different parts or personalities of the same person impacting on relationships? Does the little boy in him become attracted to the little girl in an adult woman and thus play a role in determining if the two adults start a relationship? Are they at their best when the two "littles" come out to play? Is it the teenager in the man that determines the actions of an adult male chasing after much younger women in pursuit of sex and companionship?

While these are rather simplistic examples of the existence of our child-like selves, the manner in which they may affect our behaviour as adults and influence our decisions, the impact of the neediness exerted by that piece of us that represents the wounded inner child can have serious consequences for the quality of life we experience in adulthood.

Through the normal process of teaching children the requisite social skills, parents and other authority figures deliver a steady menu of punishment in the form of disapproval, retraction of freedoms including deprivation in many forms, in either one or a combination of mental, emotional and physical abuse. In attempting to learn self control children develop feelings of inadequacy, guilt, shame and a sense of not being good enough. Children easily absorb these messages as they look upon their caregivers as an experienced person, infallible and who has their best interest at heart. How could they ever be wrong?!

Physical, social and emotional interaction during our formative years are crucial in the development of neurological, mental and emotional growth. A child needs emotional stability and physical touch from a loving hand in order to prosper.

In those formative years, the child who does not receive what is considered a standard, acceptable degree of care, receives... something else. What that child receives will be interpreted in one of two ways. Either the child comes to believe that the abuse they receive is in fact the normal experience of love meted out by the caregiver or they at some point believe that they are unworthy of a minimal standard of love and care, and deem themselves to be worth-less. This mutated sense of their own reality sets the course of behaviour to be acted out as adolescents and adults.

Recalling the earlier definition of someone who has an addictive personality, we now discover that not only does the addict act out in the form of extreme behaviour, thinking and emotions, but there is also the extremes to which one person or another will attach themselves in an effort to express their existence.

Some people will seek to continue to receive the abuse to which they were exposed, while others will seek to obtain positive messages and experiences they were denied. In both scenarios, the path to which each become dedicated will serve to determine the kind of relationships into which they enter.

Each child has a need to be mirrored. We need to see our self reflected back to us by adults. This helps us to understand that the parent understands what our needs are and that our needs will be taken seriously, and will be met. When this is not done, we begin to develop in an unnatural manner.

*****

Coexisting with our childlike ego state within us is that part which reflects the parent or caregiver who influenced the thoughts, emotions and behaviour and our interpretation of ourselves and our environment.

As we grow in age, there comes a point where we parent our self. Each of us at some point in our development, will assume the role of parent to ourself. We become the parent to our self that we experienced in our family of origin. We assume the same role and methodologies of parenting ourself as our parents did when we were young enough to have them make decisions on our behalf. We will treat ourself and perhaps others, as we were treated during our formative years. We give to our self (and sometime to others) what was given to us.

Many refer to this ego state as the critical parent.

If our parent judged us, abused us and minimized us, we may be predisposed to treat ourselves and others in a similar manner. In some scenarios, we criticize for the sake of being critical. Those closest to us may voice an opinion that we always find the negative in everything and use that as an excuse to belittle and criticize. Often that voice is our own. We wonder why others are inept and no one else can do it either the correct way or our way, which is usually one and the same. We busy our self with pointing a finger at others, oblivious to the fact that there are three fingers pointing at us.

In criticizing others we are acting out the embodiment of our parent and replacing our own self, whom we have come to believe is worthless, with attention focused outside of our self onto other people.

They are substitutes for that child within us, who is lacking and of whom we are ashamed.

Of course if we received love and validation from our parents, we may grow to mirror those attributes when directed inward and in our relations with others.

In many groups of young people there are those who seem mature and easily assume leadership roles. In a positive setting these are the children who were nurtured and to whom merit was given. In negative surroundings, these are the youngsters who learned how to use others for their own needs, one of which in this case would be to be valued.

In our formative years we were often admonished and scolded to "not do this" or "not do that". In most cases the instruction was given as a means of keeping us from harm, such as a busy street or a hot stove. Unfortunately, the reason for which it was given was not the manner in which it was received. Most children perceived it as a threat from the giver and not that from which we were being saved. We experienced our parents as being critical and having little confidence in our abilities. In other cases we perceived the world as a harsh and dangerous place. We did not understand that they were merely trying to teach us how to protect ourselves.

The conflict between the parent and the child residing inside a dysfunctional adult can be confusing at best and tumultuous at its worst. When the parent becomes critical of the childlike behaviour being acted out by the adult, the child within may experience feelings of guilt, shame, fear and any other numerous emotions tied to the experience of growing up in a similar environment.

More often than not, a cycle erupts that has the inner parent and inner child in conflict, using such phrases as "you don't deserve to be treated with respect", "no one will ever love you", "you are worthless".

The inner parent rejects the child within and the inner child through the adult, rejects the inner parent.

When activated the childlike tendencies may force an adult to experience similar feelings of unworthiness, deprivation, guilt and rejection leading to inappropriate behaviour at inappropriate times.

It is this unconscious need to act out that drives an adult person to engage with personality types that will perpetuate the environment needed to continue the same reciprocal behaviour once experienced in our formative years.

When we, as children hear a name that is consistently applied to us, we learn that is who we are... or what we are. We are labelled! We develop an image of our self which over time with repetition becomes firmly ingrained in our psyche. In relation to behaviour, a child's natural inclination is to become repetitive as it helps the child learn. Congruently, the child will learn about himself/herself through the repetition of others actions and speech. As an adult the child repeats an action or inner thoughts designed to substantiate the message that they learned in their formative years. If a child was made to feel inadequate and shameful about who they are, they will in adulthood seek out others and create an environment that will reinforce this message of being worthless, even if it is inaccurate.

A person may subconsciously choose to mate with another person who is acting out in childlike behaviours or may engage with a person who acts in a more parental nature. The "parent" will then be in a position to perpetuate the taking care of the childlike adult or conversely continue the abusive criticism and harm that the childlike adult received in their youth. Further, the childlike person now has an adult figure they can retaliate against and begin to feel some measure of relief for all the extreme negativity heaped upon them when they were young.

The manifestation of either scenario between adults is a recipe for disaster and will constitute the beginning of a damaging and emotionally upsetting relationship. Better it is that two adults recognize the underlying ego states residing within each of them and accept and manage the disparities, while building a healthily defined relationship

However, it is not all bad. Many among us did not suffer, in youth, the pain experienced by others in their growing years. Nevertheless, a childlike part of our ego remains in each of us, and it will require opportunities to exert itself. If that child within us is denied that opportunity, confusion from the suppression may result in behaviour deemed inappropriate for adults.

*****

As previously explained, the child and parent ego states reside within the adult and influence thoughts, feelings and behaviour. The extreme vacillation acted out by a codependent adolescent/adult has been well exemplified. Another point worth mentioning is that there are two extreme ends of the spectrum, either one of which a person could find them self in residence at to which they then become attached in order to act out the extreme behaviour that exists within.

In the life of many adults there are occasions whereby the child and parent ego states work in concert to help the person overcome hurdles on the pathway to success or in other circumstances, totally in line with the extreme nature of a dysfunctional addict, they work together to disrupt success and engage in self-defeating behaviour.

We previously learned that the child and parent ego states work in conflict to each other. Let us now focus our examination of dysfunctional individuals and the role in which the formative years have influenced, to scenarios that allow for the two ego states to work together, once again to assist in the development of, or to disrupt, the efforts assigned for success.

Before we can examine the roles individuals act out in concert with each other, we must first look at what on the surface seems to be a contradiction in terms. There are two very simple yet opposing clichés used to describe the hopeful formation of a successful relationship - "like attracts like" and "opposites attract". When applying these to people who suffer from codependency it is easy to imagine how each can act out to the advantage of one or both participants.

A person's inner child may subconsciously seek out a partner that will serve as their parent and provide the ability to assume the role of the "good child" in an effort to rectify the worthless feelings brought on by the abuse they suffered. Alternately, the person's inner child will seek out a partner who will act out the "parent" role so the person's inner child can fight back. Something that was impossible to do when growing up in their family of origin.

It is worth noting that the person doing the seeking could also be the person with the "parent" persona seeking to have a child to abuse or to love, depending on their own needs emanating from the unmet needs experienced in their own home.

The scenario that speaks to "like attracts like" becomes real when an angry "parent" seeks to belittle and abuse the inner child of an adult who seeks abuse because it is familiar and has been confused for love.

When a nurturing "parent" figure mates with a partner whose inner child seeks the love and appreciation that was absent when growing up from birth, the relationship has potential for real love, survival and healing at many levels.

Many people who were the recipients of messages informing them of their deficiency and inadequacy, used that message as a motivational tool to achieve success and in so doing prove that they are in fact worthy and insightful and capable. Many go on to achieve great success, some in spite of huge obstacles, usually erected by their own ego states in an effort to thwart their efforts. Others succumb to the obstacles erected by both the parent and child ego states. The parent reminds them that they do not have what it takes to be a success and the child will parade out the feelings of neglect, fear and abandonment to inspire feelings of doubt and lack, in an effort to conclude a self-fulfilling prophecy.

Many adults when questioned, fail to admit that their upbringing was less than stellar. They cannot bring themselves to acknowledge the fact that their parents were not all they would have wished for. Many who suffered abuse deem it to be disloyal to reflect their parents in a bad light. Many of those same people are afraid that some frightening event will befall them, even when the offending parent has long since died. This is the control that the parent continues to exert over the adult son or daughter through the child and parent ego state existing within.

How we were raised and the environmental stresses and parental pressures we experienced, served to shape the child and continue to exert formidable influences on behaviour within ourselves, and with others, as adults.

However, possessing child like qualities and those of a parental nature is not a weakness or flaw in our character. Each of us has a child and a parent inside, and if we are not in touch with these elements of our real self, we are losing out on experiencing a piece of who we are.

When there is a conflict within us it is many times only the confusion we experience due to the disconnect between our child ego state and our parent ego state. We can help our self if we examine the nature of those two personalities and seek to have the conflicts resolved so we no longer sabotage ourselves and the relationships we have with those around us.

Outlines & Details

1. *Is there a person or situation in your life that you are trying to control? Why?*

2. *What are the benefits to you of this controlling behaviour?*

3. *How is the other person benefiting by your attempts to control?*

4. *What would happen to you if you stopped trying to control the situation or person?*

Chapter 6

Rules and Messages

For most children growing up, life was a maze of rules and messages. There was a structure embedded in our lives that served to guide us. Whether that guidance was a positive force and whether those messages served to inform us and help us develop into healthy, secure, independent thinking individuals is the question.

In most households the rules usually favoured the person in charge, the person who made - and often enforced - those rules, and that most certainly, was not the child.

In the households run by a codependent parent, the rules would by nature be a list of negatives. That is to say, the rules normally started with the words "Do not". There was little balance, if any. The person who sets out to control and manipulate, is a person who by their very nature is engulfed in negative, because of the constant sense of fear that exists within the thinking and actions of that person, in relation to their experience with the world around them. As a consequence, that fear is played out in the rules given to those over whose charge they have been given.

The following is a list that represents many of the common rules found to be the guiding agenda, by which children are often told, threatened, coerced and manipulated into following. It is by no means exhaustive.

Don't express feelings

Don't argue

Don't talk back

Don't question authority

Don't be curious

Don't listen to others

Don't pay attention to your own needs

Don't be aware that you have needs

Don't communicate

Don't trust

Don't try to be independent

Don't think for yourself

Don't show off

These rules were made and enacted to ensure the addictive parent maintains control. Not so much that they need to control others, although that is a major incentive. The rules are there to assist the addictive parent knowing where the compass is pointing at all times. Like any other person who suffers from an addiction, the codependent person must know where all the levers are, so that they know that their world has some sense of stability. They are afraid of change/growth/new. They must have what they need in order to feel safe and change is not something that provides stability. As a consequence, their life and the lives of those around them must never change. Great amounts of energy are exerted to maintain the status quo - for better or worse. For the children in the home it is always the worse, never the better! Children growing up in homes that have a codependent parent are the unintended victims of a fearful addict, who is acting out a very common human trait... fear of the unknown, in an extreme manner.

Many of the rules that govern a child's life, and those who seek to implement those rules, make an enormous contribution to the dysfunction a young person experiences and the ensuing training that occurs. Children are taught obedience to authority and are often punished for questioning that authority. This leads to obedience without content where further suppression of emotions is experienced. Rules, roles and structure are needed to maintain a level of civility.

When the roles and rules are skewered from the start and those responsible are acting out their own dysfunction created by their own woundedness, a healthy emotional outcome for all those involved is impossible to comprehend.

A young boy is told by his father to stop sniffling and that he will not be much of a man if he cries. The boy's spirit becomes wounded and when the abuse continues, at some point his spirit becomes broken as he suffers from a spiritual wound caused by the lack of emotional nurturing. The boy goes on to create a lie, a delusion. "I'm always strong. I'm always big. I don't need anyone."

When a child is exposed to rules and messages that are based on fear, shame, denial, guilt, limitations and doubt, what are we to expect of that child as she/he grows into puberty, adolescence and adulthood?

Therefore the question now becomes, "how does that person break free of the mental and emotional chains that bind them?"

After arriving at the conclusion that all is not what it could be and that there must be a better way to get through life, we can make a new set of rules.

However, on what foundation are these rules made? With little or no experience in making our own rules, how can we know what rules to make and if they are the correct ones, and what if they don't work, and what rules do we want? So many questions! Relax. Take a deep breath and allow yourself to know that the first rule is that it's ok to make mistakes. It's ok to go back and make changes.

*****

As children we are bombarded with messages that inform us of our inadequacy. We are told to "be quiet", "go outside and play", "stop asking so many questions", we are picked last or perhaps not at all in games with other children, our ideas are dismissed and we are on the receiving end of a myriad of other belittling experiences that engulf us. Even those of us who may have been overprotected, may acquire a feeling of inadequacy when we begin to question the very reason for our protection and the intense attention to which we are subjected.

The delivery of such messages continues into adulthood and in fact throughout life, if we choose to acknowledge their existence. For examples of this, with an objective eye, just watch television for a few hours and witness the number of advertisements that seek to convince us of how weak, sick and ineffectual we are and will continue to be, lest we obtain that certain product that will restore us and in fact allow us to become better then we could have imagined without the use of the said product. Yes, I know it's a marketing ploy, but I'm referring to the underlying message that is used to convince us of the need for the product, thus making a contribution to the profits of the companies involved in the strategy. The frequency of these message which is constant, plays on the mind of people who believe that they must be inadequate in some way and buy into the notion that the product will empower them. Since the person already carries a feeling of being "less than", which has its origins in childhood, it is a natural step to continue the thought or feeling process when confronted with what seems to be reality and a logical argument mounted by the seller of such products.

The imprint of the messages we receive through years of being told that "we are lacking", influence our behaviour, our thinking and our emotional output far beyond any decisions we will make as a consumer of goods and services.

As a culture, we seem to have for many decades been sliding into a singular mindset of negativity and criticism. Many people are more attentive to what is negative than that which is positive. One only needs to examine the structure of broadcast news whereby all the worst of humanity is paraded each and every hour. Notice how at the end of the hour, the presenters squeak about a playful, entertaining report consisting of a feel-good story provided to leave us with an uplifted sense of the awful world to which we were just exposed. However, the nice fireman coming to get a grandmothers pet cat down from the tree is hardly what constitutes "breaking news".

Bringing this into a more individualised realm, people worry more about what negative things may be said than any praise they may receive. A large number of people in a society believe that praise is used to manipulate their feelings, leading toward controlling their actions. Many of us were taught as little children, that criticism was more about the person who is delivering the unkind words than it is about the intended target. Remember..."sticks and stones will break my bones but names will never hurt me". Unfortunately this seems to only have been applicable outside of the home area and used when confronted by our peers in the neighborhood. It was not a weapon of defense when abusive labels were cast on us by family members we thought were old enough to know better.

As children, we more often than not accept the negative message from our caregivers, which of course will impact how we think and feel about ourselves as adults and the relationships we seek and why we seek them.

It is duly noted that people who have a healthy sense of self will avoid those who engage in negative criticism and manipulative techniques designed to covertly control.

While constructive criticism is intended to assist a person in achieving his/her full potential, and is welcomed by people who are secure within themself, there are many who reject positive critique, because they are suspicious of the intent. People who are used to abuse and are filled with fear and self-doubt, instilled through abusive parenting, will avoid positive critique, because it is unfamiliar and may cause them to have to examine their own lives.

Negative criticism is welcomed by many people, because it is familiar and they believe they are deserving of it. There are many among us who seek abusive relationships, whether consciously or unconsciously, as means of substantiating there self-belief patterns. In fact, if life seems to be pleasant and undisturbed for any length of time, they begin to anticipate disaster and they will provoke negativity to relieve the anxiety they experience in anticipating what they have come to expect as normal. They are full in the belief that they deserve nothing better!

As for the person who is delivering the abuse and control, they are merely acting out the critical parent that resides within themself. In the delivery of such tirades or in some cases more subtle and consistent abusive language and actions, the abuser may be trying to mirror or control or retaliate against the abusive parent they experienced by giving to others what was given to them.

The complexity of this depth of codependency becomes evident when we learn that while many people will stay in an abusive relationship because they believe that they are worthy of nothing better. They also believe that the apologies are real each and every time they are offered and the abuse will than stop. Of course the question that begs to be asked is "what will be familiar to them at that point?" In fact, they will be the one to abandon the relationship to seek out another abuser and continue the familiar cycle of abuse, toleration, apologies, and wrongful belief.

People seek others for partnering with the intent of having their needs met. While it may seem on the surface in many cases that only one partner is having their needs met, it is becoming clear that many relationships function in a manner that contributes to both partners resolving their needs in what ever fashion is required, no matter how perverse or dysfunctional those needs are.

Take for example the fact that two people have residing within them a critical abusive parent, a case of "like attracting like" They end up in a relationship whereby they abuse and control each other, exchanging roles of abuser and victim. On the outside it appears they have little or anything in common, as they fight and argue their way through the partnership... but on the inside they are fulfilling each other's need to control and retaliate.

Once again, the people involved in this relationship are acting in this manner out of a need to be accepted and loved. They continuously attempt to gain the upper hand in the partnership and seek to be valued and gain merit. The opposing person does in fact possess the ability to provide support, but that ability is buried beneath layers of receptive abuse and pain. They each are only capable of giving what they know. They unconsciously accept that they will remain in this relationship as a means of trying to achieve the love and acceptance that have been denied them during their childhood.

Another frequent matching of pairs takes place between adults is that of two inner children. The inner child of one person spends a lifetime appeasing the inner child of the second person in the hope of gaining love and acceptance. It makes no difference if the second person is abusive or kindhearted. In childlike manner the second person may offer threats to the first person, that revolve around feeling secure or feeling the wrath. Consequently the first person with their inner child fully in bloom holds onto a fantasy of being accepted by being the type of partner that is desirable, even if it means being the victim of abuse. The dominant thought being that they only have to try harder and be a better partner for the other person to change.

Dr. Rhawn Joseph in his acclaimed and insightful book titled The Right Brain And The Unconscious (Plenum Press-Plenum Publishing Corporation 1992) relates a story of three children who having grown up in a household that included an abusive father and a compliant mother to whom the abuse was directed, interpreted their shared experience in very distinctly different ways.

One daughter who feared her father, also had little or no respect for her mother for accepting the behaviour meted out. She believed her mother was weak. As an adult, in her own relationships she exhibited many of her father's traits whereby she was aggressive and demanding of her partners with whom she became involved.

Her sister learned that it was normal for men to treat their partners in an abusive manner with threats, intimidation and fear. Consequently she married a man just like her father.

The third child, a boy, who had contempt for his mother, also commiserated with her as she often turned to him for consolation. As an adult he entered into relationships with women who seemed inadequate and helpless and often emotionally disturbed. He was trying to rescue his mother, something he had failed to do as a child. Furthermore, in "rescuing" these women he exerted a certain amount of control while making them dependent upon him and reminding them that without him they amounted to nothing.

Each of these adult children exhibit classic scenarios of dysfunctional behaviour. That they grew up in the same environment and differed in their own codependent behaviour is not exceptional.

As mentioned previously, not all adult children act out. Many act in. That is to say that the dysfunctional behaviour they exhibit is directed inwards. A child who has been on the receiving end of constant and severe criticism will undoubtedly acquire an inventory of feelings ranging from resentment, anger, guilt, fear, insecurity and other related emotions and thoughts. As an adult, this person may come to resent themself for not being stronger and more capable of defending against the abuse and experience thoughts and feelings of hatred and rage toward their abusive caregiver. At the same time, their inner parent, the persona they have adopted as being that which they know, continues to belittle the adult and cast doubt and feelings of inadequacy into the thoughts, feelings and behaviour of daily life.

The strain of constant bickering between the two selves residing within the person is confusing and demoralising at best and precipitates fear and self-loathing at worst.

More often than not this is a recipe for internal conflict that leads to chronic depression, institutionalisation and death.

Outlines & Details

1. *Record yourself talking about the messages you received as a younger person and how those messages have impacted on your adult relationships.*

2. *Write out a list of Rules to use in your different relationships. Make the title "MY Rules" Once you've completed those lists, record the lists and keep them with you so you can listen to what you have created.*

3. *What thoughts, feelings and behaviors will the new rules create?*

4. *How will you look and sound different?*

Section III

The Other Journey

Chapter 7

Our Return to Wholeness

The successful journey to becoming whole and realizing our potential means that we must stop controlling others and learn the difference between abandonment and detachment, especially the notion that we can detach with love. Establishing boundaries and dismantling our walls as well as stepping away from denial and instead learning how to problem solve are critical steps on the path to self awareness.

We must learn how to identify our feelings and how to express them appropriately. Learning the difference between our wants and needs and becoming aware of what they are, is vital. We must stop compulsively caring for others and learn how to care for ourselves. We must stop focusing on all that is negative and start to become aware of what is positive.

Trying to mask the pain associated with having our developmental needs unmet, throughout our lives we have built an impressive arsenal of weapons designed to control others and distract attention from that of ourselves as well as others, of the weakness we feel from within.

We must now take those weapons of the past and transform them into tools that will assist us in discovering the goodness that resides within us, and help us complete our return to wholeness.

When a person suffering from codependency wishes to change their thoughts, emotions and behaviour patterns, they must come face to face with what is unknown to them and become aware of their inner child.

It has perhaps become somewhat evident that there are only three things that we do as humans. We think, we feel, and we act. In order to complete a successful journey that will restore us to our natural self, we must incorporate each of our human elements. We must modify our behaviour as it relates to how we treat our self and others. We must become aware of our actions and reactions to events outside of

63

our self as well as the self-talk that consumes us, much of it mired in self doubt and fear.

Most people seek to become accepted by whatever person or group they deem important to their own sense of self worth. In so doing they fall prey to those who would exploit them for profit, which is not in this case , measured in currency. The mistake is made in thinking that if no one loves us we must be no good. Think of the lyrics I explained about not having anyone to love you. We were taught that in order to be loved we must first love another person. To an extent, this aged old saying may have value. However, the missing piece belongs at the beginning of this equation by formulating the notion that I'm unable to love another before I love myself.

So the formula for steady love and love from a like minded, safe individual goes like this...

Love myself... love another... receive love from another.

Remember that we were taught not to look inside of ourselves, lest we be tagged with practicing narcissism, and being conceited. We learned not to love ourselves. It is no surprise that many children grow up and begin to expect love from others before giving those same people love. It's not difficult to imagine that we could not entertain some abstract notion that we could love ourselves... especially first!

In order to heal from the trauma experienced in our formative years and those events that we have experienced as adults that helped to perpetuate our helplessness, our woundedness and our shame, we must travel inward to the very depths of our soul, in search of self and discover who we really are and reconnect with our inner wounded self. That self who was abandoned by our caregivers and ultimately by the person whom we have grown to become. We must get in touch with our emotions! We must connect with that wounded child that resides within us.

It is not an easy task this journey, and in many ways it is an emotional minefield. To secure our place in a new world of emotive action and thought, we must commit to having corrective experiences. We must be conscious and vigilant in our work that we will not see ourselves pulled back into the dysfunctional system that harmed us and from which we seek to escape.

Some adult children are angry! Angry at their parents and caregivers when they begin to realise the nature of the abuse to which they were subjected. Many others are merely filled with a sense of sadness and despair upon realizing that they have missed out on a very real and important part of their lives and the subsequent upheaval.

We must not blame our parents and authority figures. We have to instead see them for the wounded people they were. They only gave to us what was given to them, or perhaps what was missing from their own development experience. They are not at fault for not having all that was needed to give to us.

It is difficult for abuse victims to come to terms with the notion that their abusers were in the majority of cases acting out of their own woundedness and dysfunction. What seemed like premeditated acts on the surface which is what they were, came from a deeper need that was stuffed so far down inside that it only manifested through intense pain suffered by the abuser who acted out his or her own woundedness in what in many cases were perverse and damaging acts.

When a male aged in his twenties breaks into the home of an elderly women who has already passed her eightieth birthday and commits sexual abuse, it is not about a natural inclination towards arousal. It is about power! The male is only interested in gaining and exerting power over a female that perhaps reminds him of a caregiver. He acts out his anger/frustration and violence driven by an apparent need for revenge on a person who is in every other respect a total stranger.

As children we would have experienced several events that at the time they happened were so traumatic and became buried deep within the subconscious and are not accessible by means of conscious effort.

Notwithstanding the repeated incidents that shamed us and gave us fear, guilt, insecurity and other pain that we are reminded of as we act out our dysfunction in adulthood, the events can have a profound influence on our lives as adults and be the reason for much of the anxiety we experience.

The memories that have been made inaccessible to the conscious mind have become repressed. Repressed memories are memories of events that cause anxiety. While the memory may not be readily accessible the anxiety associated with the event acts itself out in our life. The memory is stored in the right brain. The language of the right brain and the subconscious is that of images. Hypnosis can be used as a safe and successful means to access the subconscious and assist the person to relieve themself of the memory of whatever traumatic event has come to influence their thoughts, feelings and behaviour in adulthood.

With the aid of a skilled therapist combining techniques such as relaxation methods, guided imagery including visualization, and free association the adult can access, interpret and analyse past experiences that are hidden from conscious thought, yet impact us each and every day.

To this end we can affect the most unpleasant and untouched memories associated with our inner child and inner parent. We become masters of our own lives and begin to realise a sense of balance leading to harmony.

Many people who have suffered a life of victimization are now recovering from the abuse that was received and are enjoying a life of developing interests, curiosity and achievement. Some may find themselves in a group therapy program from substance abuse while at the same time receiving counseling for their issues related to codependency.

The broad strokes needed to embark on a program of self awareness and discovery are a change in perception and a change in the way we think and act. The change in feelings will follow when we invoke different thinking and acting patterns.

We must drop our expectations of others while lessening those we have of ourselves. A bit of self observation will reveal that many times when we harbor expectations of others we end up either being disappointed that they did not meet our expectation that we set for them, in order to please our own sense of who we want them to be... or we try to control that person to act in a manner that would then meet our expectation. Both of these scenarios is full of defeatist behaviour, and applies unwanted and unnecessary pressure to the other person as well as ourselves, resulting in anger directed toward the other person, because they were unable or perhaps unwilling to do what we wanted them to do, to make us happy and allow us to feel justified in being able to "predict" their action. Conversely we often feel justified in feeling angry when they have not met our expectations. Many people will begin to think that if the other person really cared about us, they would have done whatever was necessary to meet our expectation of them. How dare they fail us and leave us disappointed.

Many people suffering from an addictive personality, or a codependent nature, have spent the better part of their lives trying to survive and as a consequence have had little if any experience in knowing what it is to truly be living. There may have been the odd moment or event that allowed them to glimpse what for many was a foreign way of life... a strange yet somehow wonderful sensation informing that there was more to living than the daily drudgery of existence. Those people have been enduring life... not living it! However, as we begin to experience an emotional thaw... as we begin to feel our feelings and allow ourselves the safe expression of those feelings, we begin to experience a bit of living, life without burden, at least without all that we had carried. We discover that living is infectious and we want more. As people with an addictive personality, we are addicted to more... and more of what feels good instead of just what is familiar.

For others, still unable to break free of the chains that bind, we see them still wrapped up in negative energy, dancing with the old devil, the familiar devil instead of any possible new ones.

Those who embark on their journey start new relationships and end others. We learn to set goals, small ones at first. As our confidence grows, we set goals with bigger impact and we gain confidence in ourselves and others who reach out to help us. In all of this we learn a new set of skills. We learn how to take care or ourself.

One of the early skills we learn is not to beat ourself up when we fail at our new attempts to live a real and meaningful life. We are't perfect and we never will be. We can do better, but some days... we just might do what we know best... we survive. This is when we learn about being patient.

For those who are people pleasers and caretakers, a feeling of guilt or shame may engulf us when we say no to a person who previously would have pulled our triggers. We may feel bad during or after we set up a boundary... but we do it, knowing that the old behaviours and old feelings lead us down a trail of self destruction.

Boundaries are the limits we place on acceptable behaviour of others and ourself. We have different boundaries with different people regarding the same issue.

A boundary establishes where a person begins and another person ends... or where a person ends and another person begins.

Children who were victims of mental, emotional and physical abuse had these boundaries violated. They grow into adults not knowing boundaries. In many situations there are boundaries but they are distorted and unhealthy.

In the process of healing from the trauma we learn to set boundaries. We remember that it is about us... not about another person. We can't stop others from trespassing and ignoring our boundary, but we can modify our reaction to the trespass. We can only accept responsibility for ourself and we can only construct healthy boundaries fir ourself.

As we were erroneously taught that we were responsible for other people's feelings, and conversely, they are responsible for ours, is it no wonder we have difficulty establishing proper healthy boundaries?

Many people have great difficulty defining their responsibilities and feelings. They become confused when asked to draw that mental and emotional and even sometimes physical line between themself and others.

As we grow in our own awareness and our place in the bigger picture, our ability to establish boundaries grows. It becomes easier and we feel safer in setting boundaries and asking others to respect what we are doing. Establishing boundaries helps us grow because we must act in accordance with the boundaries we've set up. Our deeds must match out words. Establishing boundaries provides us with another opportunity to mean what we say, and say what we mean.

*****

Intimacy

Establishment of boundaries is the preparation for intimacy. Intimacy is much more than sexual in nature. Intimacy is the closeness two or more people share when they are engaged in an activity of mutual consent with a mutual goal as the finished product.

Understandably, for may people the effort to engage in intimacy is seen as a risk. Having spent a lifetime detaching from one's self in an effort to not feel pain or falsely believing that the abuse they were suffering was in fact intimacy, because they were told this lie and thus carrying out further self abuse and inflicting abuse on others, it is easy to comprehend the difficulty and hesitation experienced by a person who is engaged in the healing and recovery process who is now moving toward real intimacy for what may be the first time in their life. They can be forgiven if they don't get it right the first time... or even many times after that. Who among us gets real intimacy correct each and every time?

Unresolved issues and unfinished business prevent us from achieving intimacy with others and stunts our growth and awareness. A healthy trust and acceptance of ourself and others are two of the main elements contributing to healthy and satisfying intimacy. We can only trust and accept others to the degree to which we can trust and accept ourself. We must know that we can enter and exit safely and with dignity, and conversely, we can allow others to do the same. Expecting to prolong intimacy is unreasonable and may point to yet further unresolved issues surrounding a need for attachment and fear of abandonment.

Abandonment issues, an issue with many adult codependents must be healed prior to the development of healthy intimacy. Controlling caretakers and people-pleasers are not candidates for intimacy, yet many people attract or are attracted to this type of person and mistakenly feel that they can share themselves or will be shared too by the still practicing dysfunctional codependent.

Further, people who act out obsessively are not able to share at a truly intimate level. Of course people who feel shamed are unable to experience intimacy. We must be able to accept ourselves before we can be accepted by others. When we have a believe that we are not alright we will not share ourself with others. If we have no teaching, no knowledge, if we have not experienced real intimacy, we are unable to enter intimacy with others, not out of desire, but rather out of ignorance.

In order to have successful intimacy there must exist in all parties involved, strength of character and mutual and self respect. There must be a comfort level that allows each individual to feel that they can be who they are at any moment and not be rejected or abandoned. A certain amount of surrendering is what takes place in the exercise of having and sharing intimacy. Intimacy is not so much about loving ourself or others, it's about allowing others to love us and feel safe and comforted while immersed in the process.

Outlines & Details

1. How do you feel about change? Do you think you can change? Why or why not? What do you think would happen if you begin to change? Write in your journal explaining your answers.

2. What are your patterns of self-neglect?

3. What are some of your favorite self-care activities that help you feel good about yourself?

4. What are some of the people, places and things you enjoyed when you began your recovery from codependency. Have you stopped doing them? What is your rationale for stopping?

5. What activities help you feel peaceful and comfortable?

Chapter 8

Historical Work
Where it began and why

The cliche that speaks about the necessity of knowing where we came from in order to get where we are going is applicable on the pathway to healing and self awareness. A complete program of owning our history, while not taking ownership or accepting as our fault the reason people abused us or the abuse we heaped upon ourselves, means we must examine our feelings about the actions of others and ourselves; the messages that we accepted and transmitted; the patterns into which we fell and the people involved in our lives that contributed to our codependency. There is a lot of "unfinished business" to which we must attend... but easy does it. We didn't become codependent in one day, and we will not get better in one day. We take the necessary steps and we move forward. We must bring up all of the fears, the guilt, the shame, the pain. We must get it out, grieve it and let it go. It is about the journey, not the destination!

When we were growing up, we were told that nothing is inside of us, that it is all out around us. It was implied that if we went inside of ourself we were conceited or narcissistic. As a consequence of this training, we find it difficult to look inward. This was one of many messages that kept us from knowing who we were. It is the impact that this message has on us that makes the journey inward very painful, and frightening. However, we must remind ourself that it is the journey inward that will release us from the chains that bind and that it is necessary to travel at a pace that will differ in speed and allow us to feel safe and comforted.

For many people, after realizing that they can improve the quality of their life and it can become manageable and admitting that they have no power over others, the journey begins with a look at how they got where they are. They examine the roles and rules that dominated their upbringing inside of their family of origin.

Many of the more important issues involve working through unresolved issues and feelings. Examining who had control, and was it overt or covert?

Many adults who suffer from their own codependent tendencies remain influenced by the abuse they suffered in their formative years. Perhaps they were not allowed to play and be curious as the natural inclination of childhood would provide? Frozen feelings is a common issue suffered by many adult codependents... especially males! Many children, who were denied their inalienable right to a childhood, were the victims of abuse, and because there was no safe outlet for the painful feelings they experienced, they froze those feelings. Such an experience, repeated over many years growing up, has trained us to not feel, not to be aware that we have feelings and certainly not to express them if we connect with any emotion inside of us. As a consequence of this training, we have learned to bury and stuff our feelings further and further down inside of us, where they eat away at us, on an emotional, mental and physical level.

One good example is the guilt we may experience because we hold contempt and fear for our caregivers. While we feel justified in "hating" a parent, we become confused as the message that informs us to love and obey them conflicts with our original emotion. So with the confused and conflicting emotional battle raging inside of us, many do what they trained themselves to do... they freeze that feeling. They stuff it inside, where it can be buried and ignored. This is a coping strategy that worked for many children and is a behaviour pattern that is carried into adult living. It is a survival mechanism.

However, in adulthood, being cut off from our feelings, the knowledge of them, and the expression of our emotions, will undoubtedly have consequences in our attempts to build relationships of all kinds, necessary to enjoy and maintain a quality of life to which most people aspire.

So we must ask ourselves… what are the rules and roles in which we find ourselves as adults, that are directly related to the situations to which we were exposed as children which continue to dominate us as we grow older?

Outlines & Details

1. Perhaps there are events from your past that you often find yourself thinking about. What are they?

2. Have you dealt with your feelings about these events? If not, why not? If yes, what benefits were realised?

Chapter 9

Emotions

Emotions are just energy in motion and provide an excellent guide to the centre of our Being. It is our emotions that make life both meaningful and painful.

Remembering that codependency is beset with extremes, it can be no surprise to uncover the realization that while some people are dripping in the expression of their emotions, others have bottled up and hidden their feelings to the world.

Those who have not had the exhilarating experience of expressing emotions may have lived that way because they were taught to keep it all inside, or that their feelings didn't matter or perhaps they were simply not instructed on how to express what they were feeling, and rather than make a mistake and be embarrassed, they kept it to themselves.

Those who freely express themselves may be acting on the ease with which they interact with others and may see their abundant forthcoming as perfectly natural and perhaps a cultural norm. Many people may be using their expressions as a means of control or have not enjoyed the education that would allow them to understand the discretion required when in the company of others.

Emotions must not be used to control or dictate the feelings or actions of others, nor can we allow our feelings to be ignored.

During the process of recovery from codependency we must acknowledge our feelings, as varied, confusing and many as there will be. We accept that we are human and in so being we are allowed to have and appropriately express our emotions. We use ourself and our own feelings on which to practice being non-judgmental, non-dismissive and unafraid. We must learn how to accept not only our feelings, but the accompanying thoughts, and accept them all, without repression or censorship.

If we find that our feelings and the accompanying thoughts are overwhelming, we are provided an opportunity to practice not having everything in an instant. That is to say... we don't have to react instantly. We can allow ourself to detach from the need to provide an instant response. We can wait! Yes wait! We can wait for an hour or a day, until we have had time to become used to the feelings and thoughts, the information that provoked the feelings and thoughts and allow time to process all of the information, including a response, if in fact one is required.

For those people who have no hesitation in expressing their emotions, this formula provides an opportunity to check that the response is appropriate and the sense of emotions they are experiencing is correct in the unique experience.

Those who have little or no experience in the expression of emotions will enjoy the process of the formula as it helps to assist them in feeling safe in exposing a very tiny bit of themselves to the world and their immediate environment.

This process is not done in isolation. It is often better to share preliminary reactions and emotions and thoughts with people who are deemed safe individuals with whom we can seek participation in helping us toward a better understanding of ourselves.

Denial

Denial occurs when we unconsciously alter reality. As children, we may have not been allowed to use all of the information available to us or a distorted picture of events was presented. Working through denial is a process of recognizing and stating our own truths. Truth brings freedom. Learning to learn how to do this is the first step. Surrender is the key principle to working through denial.

Emotional surrender i.e.: "I am feeling... " or "I am unable to feel... ."

Mental surrender i.e.: verbalizing the distortion, the crazy making inner picture to a safe knowledgeable caring person, one who assists in self-exploration of another.

Denial is lying to oneself about the pain, because of distorted thinking.

When the pain of childhood becomes traumatic, our innate ability to survive takes over and the child disassociates. The child separates thinking and feelings. The mind says, "this is not happening to me". The emotions become suppressed.

A large part of denial is delusion. The untruths we learn to separate inside of us, become the reality in which we find ourselves. When in denial, one changes one's behaviour to accommodate the experience.

The Codependent learns to unconsciously change reality, which is the first response to pain. The codependent cannot operate out of pain and moves past pain into the denial response. They minimize events. i.e. "Oh it wasn't so bad, I didn't cry, he only hit me once!" Codependents live with their own narrow view of what they see and how they see it. They live outside of how it really is and choose to believe however they want it to be. They imprint their own interpretation to justify their continued involvement

Shame

Shame and guilt are by the measure of many codependents the most powerful emotions and are capable of keeping us grounded in old behaviours and thoughts. Shame and guilt are used to control and manipulate us.

Shame is related to who we think we are based on the messages we received through the actions of others.

Shame is rooted in our upbringing.

In the words of John Bradshaw shame is "the integration of your disowned parts". In other words, accepting all of ourself: our shame-bound feelings, needs and wants; our anger, sadness, fears and joys; our sexuality and our assertiveness. These are the parts that were split off out of shame. Writing dialogues with those parts, using visualization, dream work and ritual can help us reunite with and accept these parts.

Finally, the most important thing we can do is choose to love ourself. This is the greatest enemy of shame.

Children who were provided an opportunity to become self aware and allowed to express their natural feelings and thoughts and encouraged to become the person they wanted to become, would have experienced healthy shame. Healthy shame provides us with a sense of community as well as self and helps in building our values, ethics and a conscience. Positive shame informs us that our inappropriate behaviour is an action that is undesirable but does not identify who we are.

Shame is the fundamental characteristic of codependents. Negative shame is where it all comes from... the addiction to substances, the addiction to relationships, dysfunctional behaviour. Codependency is a shame based dis-ease. Negative shame informs us that we are not worthy and is directly related to who we are. We are known by our actions... and our actions are never good enough.

In dysfunctional families and codependent adult relationships, shame is used to control others. It is a close relative of guilt and fear. People who suffer from codependency are people who have been given shame for who they are, or who they are not, in many cases. They have been given shame for not measuring up to others expectations or desires. These people have been told that they were not good enough, not able, and lacked everything that was needed to be any type of success or to fit in.

Shame can be given overtly or covertly. It tells the person that they are not ok! The consequences of being shamed on a continuous basis is profoundly distressing. Most people who were subjected to this message live their life believing that they are worthless and lose any ambition to achieve. Many people aspire to achieve mediocrity, while many others spend their life in servitude, doing whatever it takes to gain approval from others. This often leads to a life of degradation and misery.

Many years ago in relating a story of how a client was recovering from her dysfunctional state of being, she described very succinctly the broken barrier of shame based feelings when she humbly yet firmly exclaimed that while there were things she had done in her life that she could never be proud of... she was no longer ashamed of them.

When I enquired how she managed to arrive at this state of awareness she explained that she now understood that her actions were formed from a place that existed from a completely dysfunctional behaviour born out of the pain and fear that consumed her at the time. In fact she said that the actions were those of someone else living within her body, not herself who she now knew to be a logical and rational and thoughtful person, who had been smothered and all but extinct under the cloak of dysfunction and codependent behaviour.

Guilt

There are others, that while subjected to a shaming message, have some sense that they can achieve more than they were ever given credit for being able to do. This causes confusion and doubt. Often they will feel guilty for thinking that they may be better then their caregivers and authority figures told them they could aspire to be. They doubt their own abilities and dare not believe in themself....little wonder there, as few if any showed belief in them when they were young and needed encouragement. Therefore shame, or the way in which we see ourself and how we think about ourself, can have an impact on the choices we make. If we don't think we're worthy, we often will not try to achieve anything. Furthermore, the choices we make will be those that substantiate and reinforce the belief we have about ourself. It's a cycle of defeatist behaviour, and we are made to become our own worst enemy.

From the beginning of human history, each generation has accepted guilt and in turn has passed it on to successive generations. Parents, children, friends, spouses, partners, governments, corporations religions and institutions have used guilt for behaviour modification, punishment and revenge.

Guilt has become so much a part of the fabric of our culture that it seems quite radical to suggest that it's been a mistake. But it has!

Guilt (and its relations, shame and blame) have been a plague that has cost humanity untold pain, suffering and despair. They have too often caused us to feel negatively about ourselves and to accomplish less then we are able.

Many of us have more than enough that serves to inhibit our true nature.

Guilt is about behaviour, something we do or have done. Guilt can be a useful tool that influences our decisions but can be a terrible drain of our energy if we engage it on a consistent basis.

Throughout society, much of our common shame and guilt is tied into the fact that we are sexual beings. While advertisers use our lustful urges to stimulate the subconscious, society invokes a double standard about it being unacceptable to openly discuss sexuality.

Many believe that guilt is a feeling, something that manifests through our emotional centre. However, on closer examination it's clear that guilt is a mental attribute that "infects" feelings. It's like a foreign substance that gets into or around emotions, like an infection in a wound.

Emotions, even the powerful negative ones, are meant to be felt and acted upon. Without guilt, authentic feelings can flow smoothly and move through us. We feel the feeling and then it's gone, leaving a space that can later be filled with joy, excitement, power and other emotions. For instance, grief without guilt feels warm and smooth, like love. Fear without guilt feels like excitement or anticipation. Anger without guilt feels like power.

The easiest way to handle feelings infected with guilt has been to deny the feelings. For many of us this has been crucial to maintaining self-esteem and keeping our optimism high enough to go on with life.

The problem arising with this is that denied feelings don't vanish, they submerge and stay unconscious. This creates an opening for the parts of us that experienced the feelings and are now suppressed to repeat destructive or unwanted patterns of behavior.

Denial is merely a coping mechanism. Real healing occurs only at that point when feelings are felt and guilt is confronted and removed.

Upon the accumulation of messages intended to instil shame and guilt as control mechanisms, we go on to experience any number of feelings, the acquisition of which serve only to confuse us. Some of these feelings which are of a temporary nature provide opportunities for change and learning, and we outgrow our reactions as we mature or acquire newer knowledge of the particular situation and our options in relation to the original action.

Many people wrongly believe that guilt is necessary to keep us from involving ourself in negative, unhealthy activities. A good conscience does not depend on guilt, but rather on a self-assured sense of what is proper and improper behaviour.

In many instances, guilt erodes conscience by degrading self-esteem and even causing self-hatred. Laden with enough guilt, a person can arrive to a position where they feel obliged to prove to themselves and the world just how bad they are.

It is difficult to connect to emotions that are coupled with guilt as they are denied, and are no longer available to us. In the absence of true feelings to inform us, it is difficult to achieve that self-assured sense of right and wrong that helps make a good conscience. Releasing the judgments that hold guilt in place is the key to healing

When engaged in the process of healing from guilt it becomes important to remember that we by our very nature yearn to learn. However, learning is a trial and error exercise. We often make mistakes we don't wish to repeat. So we learn. If however, in the learning process we get infected with guilt, we then experience bad feelings. Learning is part of our natural growth and evolutionary cycle, and mistakes serve as excellent feedback in this process.

We have been taught that making mistakes is unwanted and undesirable, however this is not true. Mistakes are an important element in trial and error learning, and are necessary for learning and growth. Learning is difficult enough without being punished for mistakes that are a necessary part of the process. Guilt erodes our sense of self worth. Depression is often the consequence of guilt that cannot move and are therefore suppressed or denied.

Guilt is held in place by judgments. Release the judgments, and guilt is released. Judgments are decisions and are easy to change. The key is to simply decide again. Take back your original judgment, change your mind.

It is difficult to connect to emotions that are coupled with guilt as they are denied, and are no longer available to us. In the absence of true feelings to inform us, it is difficult to achieve that self-assured sense of right and wrong that helps make a good conscience. Releasing the judgments that hold guilt in place is the key to healing.

We begin by recognizing that we can change our thoughts, feelings and actions. Once we have seen and corrected the error of our ways... we can then gain confidence in ourself and realise that our thoughts, feelings and actions do not define us.

I had the opportunity to listen to the explanation of a client who informed me of the reality of living in the extremes. On the one hand he was a very assertive and controlling individual who harboured anger. When exposed to the other extreme of his reality, he became very compliant and in an attempt to people-please those with whom he associated, he said yes to every request for action and responsibility that was thrusted upon him. In most cases, the instant he accepted the responsibility he simultaneously condemned himself for saying yes when he had wanted to say no.

During further discussion on the matter I revealed to him the origin of his need to please and the ensuing guilt and shame that occurred because he thought people would not like him if he said no. We discussed some exercises and new thought and feeling patterns he could practice that would assist him in liberating himself from the torment he created through the anguish he suffered from not being able to be the person he sought to be, and bring into his life a certain comfort level he deserved.

When we embark on a journey of self-discovery and awareness we learn that there is a difference between guilt and shame. Guilt speaks to what we did, the action, or thought or feeling. Shame speaks to who we are, the image we have of ourself and the value we put on our existence.

When we act out inappropriately and we feel a tinge of guilt, we are free to not feel shame but instead deal with our feelings of guilt. In so doing we release our shame based self and give ourself permission to alter our behaviour and the feelings surrounding those actions.

If we sense that we are receiving old messages regarding our behaviour, messages that would imprison us and keep us in a codependent cycle, we can allow ourself to simply change the message.

Fear

Many of our feelings remain with us and become a part of who we are and influence our own actions and reactions to events in our lives through repetition. When sustained over a period of time, the accumulation of pain and grief become the trigger for fear.

For codependents, all problems are rooted in the foundation of fear that we will be unloved or unlovable. This is further evidence of our developmental needs becoming unmet. The feeling that accompanies the fear of being unloved or unlovable, is at the core of our wound.

Being accepted, receiving assurance that we are valued, wanted, and loved is one of our innate desires. When we are not affirmed for who we are and for our existence we develop anxieties that produce fear. We have been shamed and falsely believe that we are unworthy of real love.

When we do not receive love from others, we must love ourself. This is a difficult proposition for many people who's idea of love is acted out in abusive behaviour toward themself and others. If this is what they witnessed or received, this is what they know.

Upon loving ourself we can then look to receive love from others. Our goal is to cultivate self-love sufficient to discern what is meaningful and valuable, while supporting healthy love of others.

As we grow and change, our perception changes. We learn to pace ourself and learn the value of deliberation when making wise and prudent decisions that are more congruent with internal values and external demands.

Our goal is to be fully present and aware, in any moment.

Our subconscious knows everything about us, and it knows that it knows. At its core is the very essence of enlightenment, forgiveness, humour, love, serenity, truth, and a perfect blueprint of health. This is the true gift of life. It represents our inner wisdom. It is a stable and ever present centre of creative intelligence.

While resentment is tied to the past and anger is associated with the present, fear is what we feel when we contemplate the future.

Appropriate fear is based on the presence of authentic danger. Inappropriate fear is based on what one thinks or feels may occur in the future instead of an actual response to the real issues at hand.

For most of us when we have been sufficiently provoked or frightened, our natural instinct kicks in and we respond with a desire to protect ourself. An example of this becomes apparent when we observe the hard shell of anger emerging in response to a perceived threat.

If we are frozen and cut off from our feelings and we pretend not to feel, or simply cannot express shame, guilt, fear, and anger, chaos and confusion will set in. Chaos and confusion are the result of conflicting messages, decisions and actions. The internal message is "I can't, or won't, decide."

**Go to http://chesmoulton.com/triangle
for an explanation of the triangle of self obsession**

Detaching

One of the more frequent behaviour patterns that require adjustment involves detachment. Many codependents on first learning of this basic action become confused and mistakenly think that detachment is another word meaning abandonment. It is not!

Detaching is letting go of the obsession to pre-plan every activity and conversation. It is letting go of the thoughts words and deeds used to manipulate others, and just live in the moment. Letting go with respect and dignity, both for the codependent and the other parties involved. Detaching with love! It provides an opportunity for the codependent to explain that while they may still care about the other person, they can no longer care for that person.

For someone who has survived and in some cases thrived from caretaking and people pleasing others, it is more than a stretch for them to imagine being able to live and maintain their life by releasing their well worn yet trusted methodologies of control to achieve their own objectives.

The truth is that they will achieve more than what they have accumulated, whether that be financial wealth, self esteem, or or other personal goals.

I often counsel those of my clients who seek relief from the burden of always having to be "on", who frequently complain of the travails of constantly having to be one step ahead of everyone else. They feel compelled to always have an answer to every problem, whether their advise is sought out, or not. This is what I tell them;

Instead of trying to control everything, pick out a few things that if they fail, will have no bearing on the quality of your life. These events would be of small significance in the bigger picture, notwithstanding the importance you would have placed on each and every thing that could have the slightest impact on your affairs. Imagine that in the past you would have gotten in the midst of whatever was happening in an effort to manipulate and maneuver the outcome to your benefit. Not a difficult thing to imagine, as it was always true.

Now imagine the approach you will take is to literally sit on your hands anytime you think of interfering with the natural outcome of events. Just let them play out and see what happens. Remember, if it all goes sour, they were insignificant items that would not register on your radar of success.

This may take several weeks perhaps just to wait for, or identify a few items that qualify. It may take a few more weeks to realise the results. This is something that can be repeated to ensure the results, were not just a lucky or somewhat altered happenstance.

Upon realizing that those events actually turned out to have as good or better result then when you were expending energy, you can now have a bit of faith and trust that there is a system in place that while not evident to even the keenest observer... works!

Next, apply the same principle to a few events that would have a minor impact on your life if they were not to end as planned. Sit on your hands when the urge to get in there and grind out a result emerges and tries to control you. When you are successful in this undertaking, which may have taken a few months, from the identification phase to the end result stage, you will begin to realise that many things have a way of working out with only a minimum of input.

Now that your faith in others or something outside of yourself has increased and you have evidence that it is unnecessary to expend huge amounts of energy to control an outcome, you can now choose bigger items that will have an important impact on your total wellbeing. Apply the same principle.

While undertaking this stage, the urge to jump into the middle and attempt to control the outcome will be lessening. Enjoy the positive results and continue to practice a new way of conducting yourself while seeking new and more productive areas in which to expend the energy that has become available as a result of your new approach to living.

Of course the caveat here is that I am not proposing that a person has never to engage in having an impact on outcomes. Instead I am suggesting that there is an opportunity to expend less energy then previously experienced. A fine example would be a person who is seeking employment. That person would be foolish to sit home and expect the phone to start ringing having done nothing to impact a favorable outcome. However, instead of trying to manipulate people and control the situation that may result in a job offer, and risk offending others, it would be a good idea to call up a few companies to advise them of your skills and go out and deliver a few CV's. Ensure that people know who you are and that you are seeking employment. Then go home and wait, the phone will ring, or a message will appear in you inbox, inviting you to an interview or requesting additional information.

Getting into the correct zone, mentally and emotionally is the key to success.

Detaching doesn't mean we have stopped caring. In fact it means we have begun to care for ourself. We have stopped the mind traveling required to maintain control of others and commenced to show ourselves some much needed attention. We have stopped obsessing and acting out in the extremes.

Instead of deploying our efforts onto others, we begin to concentrate on ourself. We become aware that we have feelings and discover safe ways in which to express those feelings. We ask ourselves, "what do I think, and what do I need to have and do to take care of myself?"

Focusing on ourselves is a strange and uncomfortable feeling, but if we want to have a better quality of life, it is something we must do, safe in the knowledge that like much else in life, it gets better with practice.

Letting Go... of the Victim

Along the way to learning how to detach ourself from others, we can practice by learning how to detach from a part of who we have become. We've learned that we no longer have to be victimized, but how do we let go of falling into the victim syndrome?

Some people play the victim as a means of gaining attention and manipulating people making it easier to control them by preying on emotions.

Others become the victim as a result of the abuse they receive from people.

In the first instance, this person has learned the fine art of manipulation and rather than expend energy devoted to overt manipulation, they have taken the lazy way of using people to have their own needs met. There are of course two victims in this circumstance; the person who is feigning victimization and the person who is so vulnerable that for their own reasons become embroiled in the act of deception.

In carrying out the act of deception, the pretended victim often turns into a person who will seize on the vulnerability of the other and begin to abuse and belittle the very person whom they trapped into this convoluted role play. They do this to exert their mastery of control and to demonstrate to themself and others that they in fact have "recovered" from their circumstances and are now strong and able... until such time as they once again seek to entangle others into a false sense of give and take, which in truth is really a scenario that involves only take, at least from the point of view of the pretended victim.

The person who is snared, usually quite willingly if they are a doormat people-pleaser and even more so if they are the people-pleaser type who is actively seeking "victims " to rescue, can also turn out to be very shrill if their overtures and assistance is not met with an appropriate amount of gratitude and glory giving.

The rescuer will complain that the pretended victim or a real victim in many cases, does not appreciate the effort and has not given the pat on the back, so needed by the people-pleaser.

When considering the act of letting go, one might imagine that for those pretend "victims" it may seem like an easy task to simply make a conscious decision to stop manipulating people by playing on emotions. Their reality is much more complicated and involves issues related to survival instincts, disregard for certain personality types, a lack of self worth, and fear.

For those persons who are caretaking people-pleasers, it is difficult to let go of being the victim as it require them to stop people-pleasing others on the way to realizing their own self worth and having confidence that others may like them for who they really are and not for what they do. They continue to give... until it hurts, as a means of proving their worth and then they become confused and angry when the deeds are not met with gracious acceptance and gratitude.

In many situations involving caretaking people-pleasers, the act of giving is not about the other person, it is about only them. The receiver of these kind acts is only a necessary prop, required for balancing the equation. Without someone to receive, there can be no giving.

As a consequence of their actions, caretaking people-pleasers become victims of their own misfortunes and because they lack a sense of their own real worth, it is very difficult for them to let go and stop them self from becoming their own victim.

Many times it is best to wait until anger and resentment sets in before trying to show them a better way. When their emotions are heightened and focused outward, they are often more able to rationalise and emote their constant predicament and become ready for change.

In letting go of being a victim we take responsibility for ourself and allow others to do the same.

Anger

Anger is one of the most commonly held and expressed emotions. In reality most people were too busy witnessing anger to be taught how to properly manage it. As a consequence of this, there are many myths related to the feeling of anger and its expression.

Many people have the notion that anger is not to be felt and certainly not expressed, especially by "nice" people. We have been taught that if we express anger, we risk being abandoned or punished in some other manner.

Many people resolutely believe that if others become angry at them, they caused that anger in the other person and it is now their responsibility to do whatever is necessary to appease that anger. The reverse is also true, in that many people believe others are responsible for our anger and the other person must rectify the situation in an effort to right any wrongs.

Further, many people believe that if they become angry at another, it means they have stopped loving that person. The reverse here is also believed whereby some people believe that love has ceased when another person becomes angry with them.

Some people associate violence with anger and use one to justify the other.

Many men were taught that anger is the only acceptable emotion they can express without surrendering their sense of manliness.

Anger is often therefore at the root of addictive behaviour associated with chemical dependence and other substance abuse.

I well remember a client who discovered that she was angry because she felt she did not get what she wanted when growing up in her family of origin. Peer pressure drove her into experimentation with chemical substances and she soon realised that drugs made her feel good, when all she ever felt before was bad... usually anger. So she continued to consume drugs and medicate herself. She mused "Why feel bad if I can feel good?"

For most codependents, expressing emotions of any type in a safe and appropriate manner is a new experience. Imagine the reluctance and in some cases intense fear associated with allowing angry feelings to surface and seek expression. In some cases, people who are recovering from years of neglect and abuse of many kinds are of the erroneous believe that self awareness means being sweet, nice and complacent all of the time. For many, this incorrect assumption provides little change form their past behaviour patterns and serves only to further confuse them in their quest to find and maintain a balance in all things.

Dealing with angry feelings can be a minefield of disaster, especially for those who are now experiencing and expressing emotions in a safe and trusting environment. Here are some guidelines:

*   Take responsibility for the feelings while examining the thought patterns leading up to the feeling of anger.

*   Acknowledge those thoughts and make an informed decision regarding the expression of angry feelings.

*   Remember not to allow the feeling of anger to take control and instead, when it is appropriate and with an appropriate person, discuss the thoughts, events and feelings of anger.

* Focus on the particular issue that provoked the anger and resist any temptation to get personal when exploring any role others may have played in the situation.

* Last but certainly not least, do not allow feelings of guilt to overwhelm and deter from doing all of the above.

Grieving

Elisabeth Kübler-Ross in her 1969 book titled On Death and Dying opined that there were five basic stages of thought and emotion that one experienced when faced with the knowledge of terminal illness.

She noted that these stages are not meant to be a complete list of all possible emotions that could be felt, and, they can occur in any order. Her hypothesis holds that not everyone who experiences a life-threatening/altering event feels all five of the responses, as reactions to personal losses of any kind are as unique as the person experiencing them.

Furthermore, it has been noted that these five reactions can be applied to the scenario that develops when a person who has been acting out in a dysfunctional and codependent manner must now face acceptance of the need for change and plan to change certain thought, feeling and behavioural patterns.

The five stages are:

Denial: This stage generally includes refusal, minimization, and avoidance.

People feel that they do not have a problem concerning their control over others. They often believe that exertion of additional energy is the remedy to the situation.

Anger: This stage relates to how people become upset when faced with the reality that there is a problem, and the problem cannot be solved by continuing on with the same pattern of behaviour, thoughts and emotional output.

The realisation sets in that they are the problem... not others. No one likes to be told about themself when it is perceived to be negative.

They begin to realise that they cannot change others and therefore must change themselves, which means new territory, which is uncomfortable at best and scary at worst. Anger is directed outward at others and the world in general.

Bargaining: This is the stage that people go through as they try to convince themselves or others that they can or will stop old behaviour patterns, of themselves or others.

In some instances this stage can be useful, such as when an individual agrees to counselling in an attempt to salvage a relationship.

In other instances, it is unfortunately more of the same, as when a women declares that she supposed if she just kept the house a bit more tidy her husband would cease the abuse. In another scenario the person might exclaim, "God, I promise I'll never abuse her again if you just get me out of this trouble."

Depression: A sense of sadness and hopelessness are parts of the depression stage when dealing with a codependent. Many people who are withdrawing from familiar patterns will experience this stage and will be at their most vulnerable.

This is a time when a great deal of work can be done and efforts to educate the person on a new way of living with new patterns of thoughts, feelings and emotions can bear fruit.

Acceptance: There is a difference in admitting a problem and accepting that a problem exists.

Admitting one has a problem is more likely to occur in the bargaining stage. Accepting that a problem exists is when a person accepts this as reality and begins the process to resolve the issue.

This stage in the grieving process is not about feeling hopeless or resignation. It is about coming to terms with a situation that requires change. It is about stopping the struggle. It is about accepting reality as it presently is and giving ourselves permission to move forward with new ideas and a new energy to do and become different.

Self Care

Self care is what recovery and discovery of ourself is really all about. We learn to have compassion for ourself and we begin to learn how to nurture and love ourself. We accept ourself for what and who we are at any given time. We accept that we're not perfect and perhaps also, we are a long way from being who and what we have chosen to become. However, we accept that we have strengths as well as weakness. We learn to feel comfortable with our thoughts and feelings and we acknowledge our behaviour.

We know that we don't have to stay the way we are and we look forward to increments of change. We take control of our life.

Self care is as much about attitude as it is about anything else. We can acquire all the skill and knowledge necessary to propel us on a road away from victimization, however, without the proper attitude all of that skill and knowledge is laid bare. We must adopt the correct attitude.

This is a great exercise to help us learn balance, as we do not want to become narcissistic if we lacked a sense of self. For those who had a superior level of esteem, we must give up our conceited thoughts and mannerisms and seek the same balance as those upon whom we preyed. We must be gentle with ourself and lower our expectations as we learn how to parent ourself with the care and attributes that were missing from our family of origin while still in our formative years.

Upon inspection we realise that we previously had an attitude... it may not of been much help as it was an attitude that was born out of shame and abuse, originating from within or given to us by others, but we did in fact have an attitude. Now we can grow our own attitude, born out of a sense of self and self worth. Slow at first, but as each day passes we become more confident and more secure in who we are and what we are doing.

We must realise that we have worth and we must grow in love with ourself. It is necessary to take responsibility for our own thoughts and our own actions as we protect our emotions which for many people will have become raw and untested.

We are the guardians over our mental, emotional, physical and spiritual needs. We must ensure that we are secure and feel safe, in all of these areas.

We must take responsibility for our choices and for change. We are able to identify our wants and needs and make distinction between them. We arrive at a place whereby we want our needs, but we don't need our wants.

We bring down the walls as we set our boundaries. We gain confidence and insight. We learn where we begin and where others end. In setting our boundaries we choose who we let in and who we keep out. We take responsibility, for what we do to ourself, what we do to others and what we allow others to do to us.

We become trustworthy and trusting. This is a huge step for many people as they realise that their trust was overridden and they may have not been able to trust themselves. Now we must trust ourselves and identify those who are safe and can be trusted. In so doing we build and maintain a thick boundary while trust builds.

Outlines & Details

1. How did your family of origin members express their feelings?

2. How do the people in your current family situation deal with feelings?

3. What would happen if you started feeling or expressing your feelings?

4. What emotion irritates you the most? Keep your journal close and make notes about what happens throughout the day, or simply make voice recordings.

5. How do you deal with anger...yours, and that of others?

6. If you have repressed anger write about it in your journal.

7. What if you could be feeling anything you wanted right now, and having that happen would be OK? What feelings would you be experiencing? Make a voice recording.

Section IV

Chapter 10
A Suggested Programme of Self Discovery

Codependency as we have learned, is for many people a deceptive and devastating problem involving themselves and people with whom they are associated, either past or present.

There is a way out and there are solutions to be offered that are simple yet specific. When applied with determination, creativity and honesty, the following steps can provide an opportunity for healing, resulting in peace, prosperity and happiness.

For many people who are more comfortable living in isolation either physically if not intellectually and emotionally, this programme provides an opportunity to engage with others. A trusted and experienced person who is reliable and knowledgeable in areas related to the subject matter is essential for a successful journey. This person may be a member of a group dedicated to healing from the dysfunctional chains that bind, or simply a counsellor whose background contains study and experience in the trial and travails of the most extraordinary journey upon which a person can embark.

The following steps serve as a vehicle directed away from a path of learned self defeating behaviours, toward a healthy and loving relationship with ourself and others. It may for many become the most arduous work ever undertaken, however the rewards are immeasurable and life lasting.

Having learned much of what made us who we are, let us discover who we can become.

While accepting responsibility for our codependent behaviours which serve only to reinforce patterns of devastation in our lives, we grow in humility. We learn of our shortcomings and defects of character and recognize our skills, talents and successes.

From this humble beginning we do all that we are able to do on the road to correcting the wrongs we have initiated, while completing the work which helps heal our wounds and those of others whom we have hurt.

These steps are written in spiritual treatment form. Each one is a healing manifestation. They are written in a very wise sense of order. The experience one realises, and manifests, as the result of the steps is one of truth, love, life, harmony, and peace known as a "spiritual awakening".

Step 1:

The first step on this journey is to know the history and understand the role we played in perpetuating our own dysfunction. We begin to understand that we are powerless and recognize the unmanageability and fruitless effort employed in our attempts to control others and keep them from controlling us.

We learn that we can control only ourself and we stop trying to achieve the impossible. We learn that control of others is an illusion. We also learn that others cannot control us.

We are provided an opportunity to identify and examine our patterns of how we manipulated, denied, and avoided, our thoughts, feelings and behaviour as it relates to ourselves and others and circumstances. We surrender to the truth.

> I know that I am human. This means I am four dimensional... mind, body, emotion, and spirit. A holistic experience.
>
> Part or all of me has for however long been unmanageable. This may mean I'm fearful, angry, living in my head-many different things to anyone. Even developed stress disorders... addictions and dependencies-whatever I'm out of control of in my life... and I need help.
>
> I admit that I am human and I need help. I agree to take and exercise my power of choice and free will. I choose to do step 2

Step 2:

Having completed the first step which provided us with a concise knowledge of our situation and the litany of abuse that we experienced, this next step gives us hope.

Engaging the help of others, we are able to examine our own behaviour and discover that the continuation of our behaviour is self defeating. We wake up to the facts and begin to form opinions. Our way hasn't worked very well. This is where the ego begins to deflate.

We begin to learn from others, share our thoughts and feelings on a specific topic... a power, divine force, loving and caring, and greater than ourselves that can restore us to sanity.

> *Before proceeding any further we must first acknowledge the modern day definition of insanity for many that has found its way into our lexicon is; creating the same thing over and over, while expecting a different result.*

Our ego learns to let go. We do not need to restore ourself, and couldn't do it even if we wanted to.

Many people mistakenly interpret this step as an attempt to force a belief in a Higher Power. This is not the case. We have now arrived at a place where we can admit that we are unable and in fact were unable to stop the abuse, right the wrongs and make our lives a blueprint of the kind of which we always dreamed.

No one else can restore us, no church, group, book, mother or father, friend or brother, no person, place, thing or event, can restore us to sanity.

Yet this very power we begin to believe "in" lives inside of us. We have within us a connection or switch we can turn on and to which we can turn our lives over to for help, guidance, and support.

All we need, will be provided for, including sanity, a sense of being okay... self-esteem, healthy boundaries, healthy coping skills and living well. A new sense of being.

We slowly awaken to a new thought process a new understanding of a power greater than ourself, one that can bring healing into our life, one that we have never been able to believe in before.

Now we do need to be careful here. Think carefully about your religious training around judgment and hell. There is no room for that here. Be very careful. This can be very confusing for some of us. This new belief system is one of love = divine love and only that which is. We have no opinion on outside issues here.

Many people may believe that their traditional image of a higher source had abandoned them in needed times. Some people experienced a belief that presented a higher power with traits similar to a tyrannical leader within their family, or community.

Others clearly believe that they were not good enough to attract the love and devotion of a loving power greater than themselves.

Clearly this is the step that will define all others from this point. All understanding will follow the clarity and stability experienced in this step.

Many people refrain from this experience which often results in confusion. or a quick return to old behaviour patterns. We are concerned only with divine love, wisdom, truth, harmony, peace, all positive and only that which is. Anything else, is irrelevant.

Outlines & Details

1. *Write out a list of traits and characteristics of a higher power with which you can have a relationship. This allows you to ensure that you have not mistakenly transferred traits that exist in an abuser, but also allows you to start forming an image of a safe and protecting higher power in which you can trust.*

Step 3:

Having admitted our powerlessness and arriving at a place where we want to do things differently and enjoy the experience of having a set of new results, we now come to that all important time of letting go of our old thoughts, emotions and behaviours.

Old Belief System - My Will

Past	Present	Future
Resentment	**Anger**	**Fear**
Hostility	**Insecurity**	**Anxiety**

Years and perhaps decades of imposing our will on others or having others impose their will upon us, may leave us with a burning desire for change, but change to what... and how do we affect that change?

For many people who were burdened with responsibilities they did not want but did not know or have the courage to relieve themselves of, this is a welcome exercise. For others who may want to give up their self defeating behaviours, this is a frightful and perilous step, if for no other reason, because as much as those behaviours have become outdated, and a contributing factor in a perceived failed life... they are familiar!

We make a decision to discover the good, the "real me", our divine self centered, higher self, co-creator. We turn over every stone of fear, resentment, frozen passiveness, anger, isolation at every level of our personality to find our true identity, our whole self. We decide to trust and take action based on our belief system.

As we continually discard our control and avoidance behaviour patterns in exchange for our new way of acting, thinking and feeling, we lift the cover from our insincerity, dishonesty, ignorance, procrastination, dependence, worry, and a lack of faith in others as well as ourselves.

We become more willing and open to continue our self-discovery process. We decide to embark on the journey within. We take off the masks. We surrender to win...to gain. We take on spiritual life.

The opposite of the system of the past in which we became enmeshed is a new belief system. A belief that if we change our patterns, the results will change.

As we begin our new way of acting, thinking and feeling, we begin to experience inner strength, to offer honest opinion, to listen, to love, and to show love toward others.

We begin to experience clarity. We would like to have and be: Friendly Comrades; have joy, smiling and laughing; Peace, contentment within ourselves and our universe; Serenity, to be at peace with ourselves and others; Forgiving, acceptance of other people's positives and negatives; Forgiving, acceptance of our own positives and negatives.

Admit =   Let go

Believe =   Belief and trust

Courage = Honesty

The old belief system was unnatural. The new system and the new process are natural.

2 ingredients to make one

A + B = C

One part human [outside] [ego] + 1 part divine [inside][self] = human being

- We are creation itself and yet not perfect
- We need to take the old belief system [my will] and turn it over to this higher power.
- If the higher power is not outside it must be inside.
- We now have an understanding. We know without a doubt that this power exists.
- Where is this loving divine power?

- Now we know what it is and are fully aware it can heal us, make us whole. .

- Made a decision (action as the affect of our new belief)to turnover our will, our life to the care of a power of our own understanding.

- We came to the opinion that we can trust, contact, and receive healing and guidance from divine love or... the good in our life and ourself.

- Our new connection a higher power, is positive and only that which is positive. It can be no other.

Outlines & Details

1. *When you look in the mirror, say something positive about yourself. Tell yourself you love you, you're beautiful, you're good at what you do. Tell yourself you're going to take care of you, and your higher power is caring for you also.*

Step 4:

Up to this point, much of our focus has been directed outward, admitting that we are powerless over others and seeking help outside of ourselves to initiate or regain some semblance of reality, coupled with a new way in which we manage our lives.

We can now begin our journey inward. We conduct emotional surgery requiring gentleness and care. We construct a fearless and moral inventory of ourselves. One that is searching and thorough, including an examination of the tools we have, our characteristics, our methodologies and actions, as well as our reactions, to our environment and those who have in the past and those who currently inhabit that environment.

This exercise is not about blaming ourselves or others. This is not a journey of guilt and shame. It is simply a thorough examination of what has happened to us, what we have done to others and ourselves. While our approach is one of self care and love, we are provided an opportunity to examine our hurt feelings and anger. We review the standards by which we have judged ourselves. In the light of our new awareness, we embrace those standards that are appropriate and cast off those which are disagreeable.

We search inside of ourself in an effort to uncover the memories of all that has impacted us. We make a list. Write it down. Get it outside of us. There is a certain magic that accompanies the entire act of writing and seeing what is in our mind, out on paper, outside of our self. In so doing, we free up space for other things, positive things, that now have room to be planted, take root and grow. The act of writing it all down means we don't have to carry it around inside of us anymore. It is a small deed related to the bigger action of letting go.

We are willing and able to look within ourself and our past to discover the negative effects and illusions, wrong thinking and damage, in order to heal our broken spirit, our divine spirit.

Some may feel this step to be a confession; this can be misleading and infers misguidance. Conduct a review of steps 1, 2, 3. Inevitably feelings come up as we make our lists; we learn to take our time, while being thorough and we love, love, love ourselves along the journey inward.

We're going to pass through dark corners perhaps or high water. It is so important to "be not afraid". The fear comes and the fear goes, as well as anxiety. They're supposed to, it's natural. A natural past response, and now we are not alone, so continue to make a list...of all we did negative to others, what was done to us by our own self and by others. We are uncovering the natural responses any human being would have in a negative situation.

In an effort to remain thorough and true to ourself, we must strive for balance and in this step balance requires us to include a list or our mental, emotional, physical and spiritual assets. Make a list of the things we like about ourself. We include in this particular inventory, our strengths, and positive contributions to those people whose lives we have touched.

This is a positive exercise about negative stuff. Trust the process not the stuff involved. Do not allow the shame, guilt and anger to become the driving force in our behaviour and thoughts. Remember, codependency is a learned behaviour, it is not who we really are, it is simply the role we played in order to survive. We now give ourselves permission to learn what it is to live. With the completion of this step we are well on the path to growth and change.

Outlines & Details

1. *Write about your relationships. Include, family members, boyfriends, girlfriends, spouses, friends, work colleagues and other significant people.*

2. *What needs has each relationship met? What have you learned, or gained, from each relationship.*

3. *For people who are not family members, how did the relationship began? If it's over, how did it end?*

4. *Are you harboring any negative feelings or resentments?*

Step 5:

Once again the exercise of taking ownership...not to deny my self from myself.

Steps four and five, for some can be a long journey and consume emotional capital. It is very important to search out another human being who has also experienced a non-judgmental process in these steps and who has clarity with positive intention, in other words a like-minded individual or individuals. However for our purposes here of finding our personality defects we shall share our list with someone who can assist us at discovering them in relationship to that diseased ego.

There have been in the past our developed or underdeveloped feeling and mental states that have controlled our behaviours, mostly all effects of negative situations from the past.

The writer verbally shares their list. At the end of this step we clearly know our nature of wrong feelings or thinking. We begin to see patterns of past behaviors, perhaps the way we reacted in our family of origin is now the same way we react in relationships today, or career and social situations or even towards ourselves. Notwithstanding the abuse we may have suffered at the hands of others, we can now safely take ownership of the suffering we brought upon ourselves.

Through the exercise of sharing our strengths and weaknesses we open ourself to the experience of new found acceptance, humility, and compassion for ourself and others. We are provided an opportunity to gain a deeper understanding and healthy respect for our powerlessness and unmanageability. Every time we withhold truth, beauty, peace, harmony, we harm or continue to harm our self and others.

So... we now take or accept help from our higher power, ourself and another to allow us to take full responsibility for ourself, our thoughts, our feelings, and our behaviors, furthering our healing process.

For many people this step needs to be undertaken with spiritual leaders, therapists, like-minded friends, and even all of the above.

Sometimes a dis-eased ego is also a damaged ego. Stress disorders, compulsive behaviours, anxieties and even phobias become manifest as the affects of our past is uncovered. Recovery is an inside job to be undertaken in safeness, security, and good humor when possible!!

This is the cleansing process, a discovery of dysfunctional humanity, however now in healing. There are divine laws under which the universe and we operate.

We seek to know the truth about ourself and live life like an open book. By doing this step we free ourselves from the past, what we thought of ourselves, what others know, and live within the commitment of true living.

At the end of this step we see clearly the nature of our wrongs or negative feelings and thinking. Many people experience a great sense of relief coupled with mental, emotional and spiritual freedom from the psychological bondage that enslaved our past. This new sense of freedom for some is immediate, for others it is a gradual awakening as we continue our journey of recovery.

Outlines & Details

1. Do you know someone who is a good listener, accepting, and non-rescuing, a person who you consider to be safe?

2. Honestly and openly discuss your feelings with that person.

3. Listen to that person's feelings without judgment or caretaking gestures.

4. If you don't know anybody you feel safe doing this with, join a support group, or get a professional therapist/counselor.

Step 6:

We are now prepared to have our character defects removed. This step in many ways is related to step two and three, in that we began to trust a source that was outside of ourselves but at the same time connected to the vey core of who we are. We must now call on that energy to help release us from the very character defects that have anchored us to destructive patterns of thought feelings and action.

For many people this can be a time of doubt and mistrust. The old ways have served well and have helped in surviving whatever abuse we may have encountered. However, we are no longer satisfied with just survival... we want to live. Once again we must be fearless... yet pragmatic. Nothing exists in a vacuum and when we rid ourself of the old patterns, we make way for new thoughts and feelings. We create space for the planting and growth of new behaviours and ways of interpreting events and people, based on what we are learning about ourself and the possibilities that exist. For every action there is a reaction - all that I give is given to myself.

Many questions arise including our commitment and ability to complete this step perfectly. Perfection is unachievable and is not a realistic goal, and was in many ways a character trait born out of our codependent past. Realising that we do not have to attempt the impossible alleviates much of the pressure and allows us to grow comfortably and succeed in reaching attainable goals.

At this point many people become distraught and lose focus, becoming resistant to change because they do not have experience in healthy behaviours and thoughts. Once again we must be fearless, ready and willing, seek guidance and proceed cautiously and slowly, building trust in ourself and the process.

Outlines & Details

1. *Is what you're emphasizing what you want to see more of?*

2. *What problems are you affirming?*

3. *What are the solutions?*

Step 7:

We must accept the notion of a power greater than ourselves. That becomes easier to do when we realise that doing it our way did not work. We continued to do the same things again and again and received the same results. That very pattern has resulted in us being here, now.

In an effort to maintain a balance we have sought to have our false pride and arrogance replaced with a growing humility. It is our humility that continues to drive us forward as we seek to have our shortcomings removed. We cannot be successful in completing this step by relying on our old patterns.

As we become more grounded in our belief and substantiate that belief with trust and faith we mature and our natural self continues to emerge. We no longer play God to ourself and others, but instead, we partner with our higher power, full in the knowledge that we cannot continue on our own. Transformation must include the energy we gain through opening ourself to something greater than we were, are, or can become.

In doing all of this we begin to have choices. We no longer have to accept our old self defeating patterns. We choose a new way. A new direction!

We speak our truth when safe, and how others respond is their responsibility. This action also takes humility. The people, places and things in which we invested anger and fear become much less powerful as we develop our own sense of worth, integrity and acceptance.

Outlines & Details

1. *How are you at making commitments?*

2. *What is you're history of commitments to people, places and things?*

Step 8:

This step is divided into two parts. First we are encouraged to make a list of all those we may have harmed. While compiling the list of people and the related actions, emotions and thoughts that were transgressed, we must also become willing to make amends to each and every one of the persons on the list.

In compiling the list we ensure that our name is included and must come first. Throughout the years of enduring the abuse we received, we may have harmed ourself through action or inaction thinking it was a means of survival or perhaps revenge upon ourself for not being able to protect ourself when it was most needed. We may have vented our rage, guilt and fear upon ourself and acted out in a self-abusive manner as a means of protecting ourself from our own feelings.

Following our own name on the list will be those people who may be aware and some who may not be aware of the trickery, manipulation, control and pervasive tactics deployed in an effort to construct an image of ourself that in many cases mirrored that of the image we were given of ourself by those who used or misused us, in an effort to establish their own misguided sense of self worth and esteem.

Guidance in making this list may come from a review of the persons mentioned in our writings from Step four. We continue being thorough and thoughtful in our pursuit of recognizing all those whom we have harmed.

While engaged in making the list we become ready and willing to make amends to them all. We prepare ourself to become accountable for our actions, thoughts and feelings. Yes we will have fears, doubts, guilt, sadness, anger and many more emotions and thoughts that could paralyze us. We take those emotions which were for many, weapons of the past and turn them into tools that we can use to propel us forward in the search for a new way of thinking and feeling and acting.

Being ever vigilant we realise that we may have to grow more and experience more healing and maturity before we can approach some people on the list. However, we do not fall back into our old patterns by using this as an excuse to avoid doing what musty be completed if we are to continue our journey.

We realize that no one has done wrong that cannot be forgiven Being egotistical is to come up short on humility. Victimisation is an allusion of diseased ego. Our true-life strengths are in the places we feel we lacked or were not given the most light.

As we begin to see our past through loving eyes we see that the things we lack the most, respect, clarity, support, understanding, our higher power had already placed within us. We were not left at the mercy of human beings. We who have received the least in our childhoods now actually have the most ability to bond

In order to complete this step we merely become willing.

> ### *Outlines & Details*
>
> 1. *How does it feel when you're around people with fixed boundaries and too many rules and regulations?*
>
> 2. *What is it like to be around people with few or no boundaries?*

Step 9:

We arrive at a place inside of us where we realise that we are not seeking forgiveness. This is not about them. It is about us! We are not engaging them for their reaction. This is very much a selfish exercise carried out with a great amount of humility.

We take responsibility to repair our soul, our relationship with a higher power. We do what we believe to be effective in each relationship to promote love, kindness, care, wholeness of spiritual self and others. We are not seeking forgiveness. We are seeking to unburden ourself from the guilt and anxiety we feel as we grow in the awareness of self reliance and self love.

We harbor no expectations regarding their reaction. We are making our amends to benefit our recovery and to assist in moving us past our old patterns of dysfunctional thinking, feeling and behaviour.

The best approach is to be simple and direct and specific. It is an exercise that presents us with an opportunity to practice our own new behaviours including humility and honesty.

A great place to start is with ourself. It allows us to experience some of the growth we seek and to practice in a safe environment. We may choose to write a letter to ourself, or to the person we were when the abuses took place. Alternately we may choose to stand in front of a mirror where we can look ourself in the eyes while we read out our list of abuses which we heaved upon ourself. We can elect to invoke the presence of our higher power or an image of who we were when we were most codependent.

As we begin to make amends to others we will without doubt encounter a variety of reactions ranging from anger to minimizing our codependent behaviours, the very actions for which we are making amends to the act of seeking to make those amends. The lack of insight by others will not sway us from our dedicated course and will instead provide us with an opportunity to practice setting our own boundaries.

We cannot make amends when doing so would bring harm to ourself or others. We must employ a bit of discretion while remaining vigilant so as not to use this as a reason to not go forward and make amends where and with who we know we can do so safely. However, we must ensure that our actions of amending does not compromise our safety or that of others. In cases where it is not possible to make amends directly, we can write a letter, after which we must decide if it is to be delivered, retained or destroyed. This decision we can make with the help of those from whom we seek guidance. In addition we can make amends by being of service to others.

We will enjoy a healing and progressive relationship with many of the people to whom amends were extended, others will elect to detach or abandon us. We will have prepared ourself for this eventuality and accept it as part of what must be.

We remember that a hallmark of our old behaviour was our inability to focus on any one event for any length of time. We started everything and finished nothing. Our challenge now is to become consistent in our behaviour and to focus on improving ourself through the process of making amends wherever and whenever possible, except when the action of doing so would cause injury to ourself or others.

Outlines & Details

1. *How does it feel when you're around people with fixed boundaries and too many rules and regulations?*

2. *What is it like to be around people with few or no boundaries?*

Step 10:

Going forward we must continue to evaluate our thoughts, feelings and our actions. We grow in ourself and mature as we cultivate a willingness and courage to admit when we make mistakes. When we are not at fault, we are provided with an opportunity to set boundaries. In setting our boundaries we learn how to protect our own sense of self worth and allow others an opportunity to take responsibilities for what does not belong to us.

Having completed this same sequence on a larger scale in step four and five, we are now ready to apply the same principle to our daily activities as a means of learning a new framework to replace those dysfunctional patterns. As many of our old habits are deep-rooted, we remain vigilant in an effort to eradicate familiar methods of conduct.

We become increasingly aware of our shame, fear and guilt. We employ the tools we are learning in an effort to own what is rightfully ours and are reminded that we can let go of these feelings. We remember to make amends to ourself and determine appropriate methods in which to accomplish this. If we are unsure about the healthiest way in which to complete this important task, we allow ourself to seek guidance. We do something that by this stage is becoming familiar and comfortable... we ask for help.

Working through the process of evaluating our patterns on a daily basis is not only about identifying what is negative that with effort can be changed. The process must include an analysis of what we are doing that promotes our well being and gives evidence to what we have learned and are practicing in our life that adds value to who we are. In doing so, we learn about balance. We teach ourself about a behaviour that was unknown to us when we were engulfed in our codependent-survival mode.

As we become more accountable to ourself, we practice more self acceptance and forgiveness. Mindful that a primary characteristic of a person with an addictive personality is extremism, balance in anything was foreign and unknown. As we now take stock of our assets, we can assure ourself that we are gaining that which we seek, stability in our thoughts, feelings and deeds.

Outlines & Details

1. *Give yourself credit for all that you've accomplished.*

2. *Write personal affirmations. Write them in a manner that is loving, empowering, that feel good when you read them.*

3. *What are your present assertions and beliefs. Listen to what you say and think.*

4. *What do you think and say about yourself...your abilities and appearance*

5. *What are your issues about money and relationships?*

6. *What do you promise yourself and to others?*

Step 11:

In acting out our codependency we gave away our power, and in many instances it was denied to us before we ever had an opportunity to know we had any. We often made people, places and things our Gods. We attributed them, or were forced to concede to them, power and importance that was far more then that which was deserving and in so doing we were left bare.

In an effort to continue our progress of recovery and to refrain from relapsing to our old negative patterns, it is imperative that we pursue a relationship with a loving and forgiving sense of a higher power as we understand that higher power. Each of us will have our own individual sense of that higher power, what it is, how it works, and how we communicate with it. In the early stages, our notion of a higher power may simply be our support network, or an individual to whom we relate. As we progress in our journey, our definition of that higher power may change, and then change again, and even a third and fourth time, until we settle on a sense of what gives us comfort and from which we receive guidance. While that higher power ultimately is something outside of us, it resides within us also, as we make an effort to make conscious contact on a daily basis.

How we make that conscious contact is our own choice, whether through prayer, meditation, conversation or some other means. Similar to allowing for a change in how we define a higher power, we allow for the method of conscious contact to evolve. In much the same way in which we devoted time and effort into changing our patterns of thinking, feeling and acting, we are duty bound to expend effort into establishing that bond and cementing our relationship in a manner that allows for growth and guidance. In so doing we become more comfortable with letting go and allowing for knowledge beyond our own capabilities to inform us, while seeking the strength, endurance and power to conduct and achieve that which is conveyed to us.

Connecting with our higher power is not only about seeking guidance and direction. Remembering that what goes around comes around, we use the opportunity of connection to express gratitude. Sending out our gratitude for whatever is positive in our life, allows for that much sought after balance to become manifested. There is no magic here, just a common sense approach to what many people were taught in their formative years... when given something positive and of value, remember to say "Thank-You".

If we previously expressed our codependence in our communications with others, it is reasonable to think that we would continue this behaviour in communicating with our higher power. Codependent behaviour can be very subtle, and therefore we must be vigilant and aware that we do not repeat these actions in our communication with our higher power. Many of us made great haste to control the outcomes of situations in our own lives and the lives of others, because of our fears and feelings. Having learned throughout our journey that we cannot control others, we now learn that we will benefit on our spiritual path by releasing our control to that of our chosen higher power.

> ## *Outlines & Details*
>
> 1   *Are you available for a relationship with a higher power?*
>
> 2.   *What are your prejudices and beliefs about a higher power?*

Step 12:

The final step in our journey of self discovery comes in three parts. We sense that we have become increasingly more self aware, we have had an awakening. We try to cary this message to others who suffer, and we endeavour to practice our new principled approach to ourself and others, in all that we do.

We have been provided a template onto which we project ourself and without regard for whatever we may believe about ourself, we know that if we just go ahead and use the template, and do the work required for progress, the result can be nothing but continued self awareness and growth.

A prime example is provided when considering a caterpillar. It uses it's own substances to construct the medium for it metamorphosis into a butterfly. We as human individuals are no less of a creature when we consider that it is possible and perhaps necessary to construct a path to liberation from within the depths of our soul, emerging after a great struggle as an expression of love, light and creation.

Our spirituality is how we allow our higher power to be expressed through us as well as an expression of our own nature. It is a vital component helping us to sustain ourself, to heal, grow and become healthy functioning vital beings.

It is important to note that we did not begin our journey seeking a spiritual awakening. We began our journey seeking relief from the mental and emotional burdens from which we suffered as a result of our learned behaviour that delivered us into dysfunctional patterns of thinking, feeling and acting. The deliverance out of darkness and into the light is what we were hoping to achieve. A spiritual awakening is merely a spin-off resulting from our own efforts.

One of the principles that we have found useful is best described through the idiom "We can only keep what we have by giving it away". To this end, we continue to carry the message that there is hope, there is a way out. The manner in which we carry that message is not one that allows us to develop new codependent patterns or for many people, to relapse back into what now would be old and outdated behaviour. We cannot force others, even those we love, to seek the path we have taken. We carry the message through the example of our own actions, our new way of thinking and expressing our feelings. We become the message! We carry the message through attraction rather then promotion.

Outlines & Details

1   What stage of the recovery process are you at?

2. What would a diagram of your recovery look like?

3. What steps have you taken in the recovery process?

4. Do you have a self-care plan?

5. Do you go to 12 step meetings or other support groups? How often?

6. Are you seeing a counsellor or are you involved with a therapy group?

7. Do you read recovery and self help books?

8. Do you spend time with other recovering people?

In Conclusion

This final spiritual treatment proves once and for all that we are free!

We shine like a lamp, a new lamp.

Now what does this really mean?

1.   We know our limits and who we are.

2.   We take full responsibility for our thoughts, our actions, our feelings and we know the "all healing" power or energy. It is at all times guiding us through the love and care we live with...in us...in our life.

We are adults, we have grown up, physically, spiritually, emotionally, and mentally and we are truly living life from within the light of our centre truth. We are linked and created to and for this process. We've done the work...received and continue to acknowledge our growth. In each step we become aware and continue to grow and change our understanding of our higher power. We have been entrusted with a beautiful gift. We accept this gift wholly and freely. As we heal ourself we heal the world!

This inward journey is the most difficult yet rewarding journey one can experience. Giving up the comfort of the pain we have lived in for so long is heart shattering and life changing, in many ways and on all levels... emotional, mental, physical, and spiritual.

To pull away in trust and courage, to not allow the illusion of abandonment to overwhelm us has been difficult work and rewarding...one day at a time.

At times we feel and think we have walked through the fires of hell and have had many crossings onto a higher understanding, bringing us closer to that brave heart, a well heart, a joyous heart and mind.

The more adult we become the more responsibility we co-share with our higher self and the more freedom our child experiences to be that which was intended... precious and free.

Final Thoughts

Our spiritual life is soul work. Let your child within lead your way; for the child, although ignorant and at times in the past lost or out of control is also your indwelling inner light, true connection to the force, your eternal flame. Let your "little" light shine!! Be happy today!!

Thank you for allowing me to share with you the most precious gift to me, for I know as long as I follow this way I have nothing to fear. Sharing with you has reaffirmed much truth in my life. Every need I have has been provided for me in my life for another day, Hope and renewal manifest through me and into my life and of the world around me. All is well in my universe. So be it in yours... and so it is!

Bibliography

Jan Fable MS, LADC http://www.forhealing.org/shame.html

Healing the Shame that Binds You
John Bradshaw - Health Communications Inc. 1988

Facing Codependence
Pia Melody, Andrea Wells Miller, J. Keith Miller - Harper Collins 1989

Codependent No More
Melody Beattie - Harper Collins 1987

Beyond Codependency
Melody Beattie - Harper Collins 1989

Co-dependents Anonymous
First Edition - CoDA Service Office, Phoenix Arizona 1995

The Right Brain And The Unconscious
Dr. R. Joseph - Plenum Press 1992

Stage II Recovery - Life Beyond Addiction
Earnie Larsen - Harper & Row 1985

On Death and Dying
Elisabeth Kübler-Ross - Simon & Schuster 1969

About the Author

I specialise in helping high achievers suffering from stress and dysfunctional relationships. Raised in families where natural developmental needs were unmet, adult dysfunctional relationships occur from the need people have to feel valued. The problem is usually related to people having an inappropriate level of esteem and confusing their wants and needs.

I hold three post graduate diplomas in hypnotherapy with psychotherapy and my name is listed on the registry of the Complimentary & Natural Healthcare Council (CNHC) here in the UK. Working internationally throughout the past 20+ years, I've successfully raised awareness to hundreds of people of the need to modify their actions and reactions to the people, places and things that impact them on a daily basis.

My business is designed to help people acquire a skill set enabling them to improve their lives through a greater awareness of who they are and how and why they became the type of person they have grown into being. I'm good at unpacking their problems so they can understand what the real issues are and how they are responding and reacting to their environment. Also, I'm able to explain where their behaviour is resourceful or inappropriate and is actually working at cross-purposes to their stated goals.

I believe that each person has the right to be unleashed from the mental and emotional chains that bind them and be provided an opportunity to experience the liberated feelings that accompany personal freedom. I firmly believe that each of my clients has the answers within. I see my role as being the person who helps them identify the layers which need to be peeled away and then provide them the confidence and security required to uncover their true self.

I deliver my solutions oriented service through the use of effective listening, focused feedback and interactive therapy. What I do is very dynamic, and not prone to intellectual chit-chat. I am redefining people's experience of what it means to have a healthy relationship with themselves and others and reshaping the way in which people view their environment.

I'm known for providing lightbulb moments and my mission is to leave people feeling liberated and confident about their future.